Extreme Ang

D0512945

A Liturgical Guide to the Sporting Year

CATHERINE FOX

MONARCH
BOOKS

Oxford, UK and Grand Rapids, Michigan, USA

Copyright © Catherine Fox 2005.
The right of Catherine Fox to be identified as author of
this work has been asserted by her in accordance with the
Copyright, Designs and Patents Act 1988.

All rights reserved.
No part of this publication may be reproduced or
transmitted in any form or by any means, electronic
or mechanical, including photocopy, recording, or any
information storage and retrieval system, without
permission in writing from the publisher.

First published in the UK by Monarch Books
(a publishing imprint of Lion Hudson plc),
Mayfield House, 256 Banbury Road, Oxford OX2 7DH
Tel: +44 (0) 1865 302750 Fax: +44 (0) 1865 302757
Email: monarch@lionhudson.com
www.lionhudson.com

Illustrations by Bridget Gillespie

Distributed by:
UK: Marston Book Services Ltd, PO Box 269,
Abingdon, Oxon OX14 4YN.

UK ISBN 1 85424 688 7

Unless otherwise stated, Scripture quotations are
taken from the Holy Bible, New International Version,
copyright © 1973, 1978, 1984 by the International Bible Society,
All rights reserved.

British Library Cataloguing Data
A catalogue record for this book is available
from the British Library.

Design by Lion Hudson plc.
Printed in Malta.

CONTENTS

(showing the liturgical sporting seasons
and major feast days)

ABOUT THE AUTHOR

Catherine Fox lives in Walsall, UK, with her husband and two sons. She is author of several novels published by Penguin, and a regular columnist for *The Church of England Newspaper*. She and her friend and illustrator Bridget Gillespie have also admitted responsibility for *How to be Perfect*, *Scenes from Vicarage Life* and *The Little Book of Vicarage Wisdom* (Monarch). *Extreme Anglicanism* is based on material which first appeared in *Church of England Newspaper*.

DEDICATED

to
Toni and Margaret Walker,
and in memory of their mothers:
May Walker
and
Grace Lancaster

INTRODUCTION

With church attendance figures in freefall it is our urgent priority to find ways of exploring and addressing the problem of secularisation. Where are the hopes and fears of the nation played out, now they no longer find their expression in the pews of our churches? Where can we still hear massed voices raised in passionate song now hymns have fallen into disuse?

The answer, of course, is in sport, and most importantly, in football. Football is the Anglicanism of sport in Britain, the default mode. If you aren't actively involved in sport of another persuasion, it is assumed that you are interested in football, albeit in an agnostic once-in-a-while kind of way – the FA Cup, say, or the World Cup.

Sport is everywhere. It dominates our national life. It erodes church attendance. What ought the Christian response to this be? My suggestion is that we follow the example of the early evangelists to these isles. If you can't beat 'em, join 'em. A hard-nosed look at the popularity of Yule in the early centuries AD suggested that banning the festival was unlikely to work. Much better, therefore, to appropriate and Christianise it. This book adopts the same approach to the problem of sport. We will never abolish football, but we can adopt its calendar and spiritualise it. Let's claim the Astro Turf!

The material that follows divides the year into the major sporting seasons (football, cricket etc) and highlights the various festival days (eg Billabong Sunday – National Surfing Championships). This is not, however, a book all about sport, any more than a year following *Common Worship* is all about ironing altar frontals. If we adopt the catholic contours of the sporting year we will find that there is room for all life there.

Given the dominance of football, the sensible place to begin our liturgical guide is in the third week of July, with the Sunday Next Before Football, or Cricket 17. This may strike some of my readers as odd, but if you stop to think about it, we are already accustomed to starting the year several times on completely random dates: the tax year on 6 April, the Anglican year some time in November on Advent Sunday, the academic year in September. One more won't hurt you.

Chapter 1

THE SUNDAY NEXT BEFORE FOOTBALL (CRICKET 17)

(Liturgical colour: white, with grass stains)

How to Calculate the Beginning of Football

In the olden days the football season used to be reasonably short. There were whole months at a time when you could sit in front of the TV without the risk of encountering a group of grown men dribbling or picking their spots, as the commentators like to put it. This is no longer true. We are living in an era of creeping footballisation of society. It is therefore our task to set boundaries, to know precisely when the football season actually starts. There are two main methods for calculating the Sunday upon which Football 1 falls.

Traditional Method: Identify the UEFA golden number of the year (in the official guide) by looking in the second column beside the first full moon *after* the preceding year's FA Cup Final. Then look in the third column for the letter, allowing for the off-side rule, and divide by 19. Add to the current year its fourth part (unless Man U are away to Liverpool, in which case, this *is* the Golden Number) and this will be Football 1. If it is a leap year, the letter found above in the official guide will be the dominical, ie from the intercalated day exclusive to the end of the year, which should mean an early away win for Newcastle United.

Mental Workout

The Sport of Worrying

A vicar I know went on the internet the other day to look up the world's Top Ten Worries. He found a great many Top Tens (Things to do in a lift, Things *not* to do in a lift, Sayings of George W Bush, etc), but no List of Worries. We found that a bit worrying. This was sermon preparation, as you will have guessed. What he found instead was a sign spotted in the Yorkshire Dales: "Any dog found worrying will be shot." As you can see, worrying can be an extreme sport.

Christian Sporting Hint of the Day

Remove your gum shield before going up for communion.

THE SEASON OF FOOTBALL

(Colour: black and white stripes)

Chapter 2
FOOTBALL 1 (CRICKET 18)

(If it should be an Olympic Year[1], this Sunday shall be designated Olympic 1. The altar candles may be lit by an acolyte in vest and running shorts bearing a large flaming torch.)

Extreme Parenting

There are many sports which fall under this general heading. It surely cannot be long before some of them are recognised at Olympic level. The demands on body and mind, the total commitment, to say nothing of the endurance levels required, make being a parent one of the toughest disciplines known to humankind. In this volume we shall be encountering stuff that makes fell-running look like an activity for cissies. Tour de France? Pff! Have you ever tried frogmarching small people round sites of historical interest?

The Educational Holiday

Being paid-up members of the Middle Class Parents' Society, a vicar I know[2] and I like to spend some of the holiday period dragging reluctant children round historical sites to justify the expense of joining English Heritage. On one occasion this took us, on a fine

---

1. These occur quadrennially.
2. From now on cavalierly abbreviated to "a VIK".

spring morning, to the promisingly named village of Battle in East Sussex. Boys would always rather be killing things digitally than trekking round the site of genuine killings from 1066, but we forced them for their own good.

Being a bit vague on my Norman history, it came as a bit of a surprise to me to learn that far from being just some dastardly Frenchie invading us, William had a pretty legitimate claim to the English throne – in the sense that he was named as successor by Harold's father and was a fairly close relative anyway. But even after knowing this, it was difficult to peel away later layers of anti-French feeling and shrug about the outcome.

As we wandered about Battle listening to our commentaries – those of us who hadn't given up on the idea and started to use our headsets as light sabres, that is – it was hard not to feel a misplaced patriotic anguish about how close it had been. (I say "misplaced" on the grounds that the Saxons were basically just an earlier bunch of invaders. This wasn't England versus France in some eleventh century World Cup Final.) *If* Harold's army hadn't just marched down from York at a rate of 40 miles a day after seeing off another invasion attempt, and *if* they hadn't fallen for the low-down dirty Norman trick of pretending to run away, and *if* Harold had kept his visor down, well, it all might have ended very differently. The French wouldn't have the Bayeux Tapestry and we wouldn't have Norman arches in Durham Cathedral.

Human history is littered with "ifs". It's only when we look back that we seem to trace a thread of narrative running through the mess of human affairs and it all seems to unfold with a relentless inevitability. Who knows what the invasion of Iraq will look like with the benefit of decades of hindsight? Will the supposed legal basis for it – the search for, and destruction of, Iraqi weapons of mass destruction – become a forgotten strand? It will all depend on who gets to write the story.

Looking out in the mild spring sunshine across the Sussex fields full of ladies' smock and daisies and cowslips, it was impossible to see this as the setting for carnage. It struck me afresh as a great blessing that it is so many centuries since our landscape was the setting for the thrashing out of these big questions of right and power.

Mental Workout of the Week: Exams

The other night I had a bad dream. For some reason I was back at school and having to sit my A-level German again, despite not having bothered to turn up for any lessons or do any work. The only positive thing to say about the experience is that it's a pleasure to wake up and realise I will NEVER HAVE TO SIT ANOTHER EXAM. We in the grown-up world do well to remember this when we are dismissed as sad and boring and old and fat. Sad, fat old bores we may be, but exams? Pah! I laugh in the face of A-level German!

Culinary Sport

Barbecuing

This is the one cooking event traditionally regarded as the preserve of men. Nowhere is this more true than Down Under. One of my sisters once saw an Australian barbecue on sale at her local garden centre. "Cooks up to ten people," it said on the label. Jeez, it's tough in the outback. If the redbacks don't get you, some mad apron-wearing Bruce will run you through with a kebab stick.

Chapter 3

FOOTBALL 2 (CRICKET 19)[3]

The Great Indoors

It is a mistake for us to think that sport is something you have to leave the home to do. The Great Indoors teems with many overlooked sporting activities. Take home improvement, for instance. This is an intensely competitive sport, with neighbours locked in duels for the honour of winning the ultimate accolade of successfully Keeping Up with the Joneses.

Interior Design

Clutters R Us, here in the vicarage. We were ahead of our time. Back in 2003, Laurence Llewelyn-Bowen (my spellcheck offers "Laurence Lewdly-Bowen", here) proclaimed, "The single most impressive interior statement for the year is clutter." If those of you with a sadly outmoded pared-down minimalist lifestyle would like to hire a crate of mixed Lego and inside-out underpants, you know where to come. Why not order a job lot of vestments catalogues, Ecclesiastical Insurance pens and dog collars for your coffee table while you're at it?

But who am I kidding? I am describing mess, not clutter. Clutter is tastefully selected and grouped items. Old pewter plates and mugs, yes. Defunct hi-fis, no. I've never been in a genuine minimalist home. Do they actually exist outside the pages of colour supplements and glossy home magazines? If so, this presupposes a whole set of people who never have to ask where the remote is, or kick a path through the weekend papers to the sofa before sitting down on a half-eaten

---

3. Or Olympic 2, see previous chapter.

sandwich. I find the idea oddly attractive. It's a bit like those ultra-posh shops with one garment hanging in the window and no price tags, and sales assistants so thin that you can't see them if they happen to be standing sideways on.

But we can all relax now and not be intimidated by all that über-chic loft lifestyle. It is so *over*. According to Mr Lewdly-Bowen, "It's bye-bye, city life…and hello to the green suburbs." I've always been a bit of a fan of the suburbs. After forays into inner urban areas, I always find myself wandering past the neatly clipped hedges and creosoted fences of suburbia with a sense of bliss. Gardens with flowers, not crisps packets!

This is not to say that the vicarage hedges are neatly trimmed or that no litter blows in our drive. In fact, during the last set of local elections I saw a Conservative Party poster on our lawn. "Pick that rubbish up, would you?" I told our older son. He stamped upon it thoroughly first. That's my boy! "And while you're at it," I said, "here's the leaflet from the British Nationalist Party – spit on it before you stamp on it." It is never too soon to encourage serious political thought in your children.

Carpentry

Does something in you die at the thought of organised sport? Well, there are other ways of keeping fit. This is what the Great Indoors is all about. A little light housework will tone up the muscles as effectively as a gym workout. But for those of you who feel ironing is for wimps, what about carpentry? Don't be daunted by lack of experience. Remember: power tools can be fun!

A couple of years ago I made some bookshelves for my study. Whenever I told people, they all said, "What – flat-packed self-assembly, you mean?" No, out of old bits of timber, I replied indignantly. "What – with bricks?" they then all asked. No, WITH A SAW AND A SCREWDRIVER! I shouted. My older son was the only one to appreciate my achievement. He referred to me for several weeks as the Queen of DIY. Two years later the shelves are still intact. I notice, however, that the study floor must be a bit wonky, as the shelves don't seem to be standing entirely straight.

"They're *not* illegal immigrants, Mrs Harbottle. They're a gift from my Feng Shui consultant in Vladivostok to improve my flow of chi."

Sporting Verse of the Week

Not all of us can aspire to the kind of physical strength on display during major sporting events. Here the Christian may take heart. God's strength is made perfect in weakness. Or, as a Baptist minister's wife I know once heard a preacher say during a sermon, "When I am weak, then am I string." I know that feeling all too well.

Chapter 4

FOOTBALL 3 (CRICKET 20)[4]

All of Life is Sport. That's my motto. Once we have grasped the inherently competitive nature of our existence, we will be able to cope much better. By now it ought to be clear that this volume seeks to explore some of the greatest challenges known to humankind. Many of these are not properly recognised as sporting in any real sense of the word. My aim here is to subvert the concept of sport and reclaim it for ordinary mortals.

Great Sporting Challenges of our Time

Maintaining your Kit

We have now reached September in our sporting liturgical year. This is the time for buying new kit or repairing the old. Here in the vicarage we go through those well-established pre-term rituals of buying new school trousers and failing to locate the crucial letter which tells us when term starts.[5] I find the trouser issue both worrying and complex. How come, for instance, one son goes through his trouser knees and the other doesn't? How come it's only ever the left knee? And is it worth attempting a pre-emptive strike and sewing a patch on now, before a hole can develop? I've ruled out the possibility of iron-on webbing, or whatever it's called. I know from experience this results in me looking at the patch, now chemically bonded to the iron, and thinking, Hmm, now that's not right, is it?

No, I think the answer is to pair up with another parent with a

---

4. Or Olympic 3.
5. Our younger son is understandably twitchy on the latter subject, ever since we took him for his first day in Reception a week early.

similar-sized child who always goes through the *right* trouser knee. We can carefully snip the trousers apart along the crotch seam, do a swap, and thriftily form an entirely new pair of trousers out of what would otherwise be thrown away! Or we can optimistically cut the bottom of the legs off to make shorts. The child will then say, "Mum, no *way* am I wearing them. I'm not a *baby*."

Extreme Parenting

Guilt

There is no doubt that parenthood is one of the most demanding sports on the planet. It is gruelling not just for the length of time the event lasts (for the rest of your life), but also for the emotional toll it takes. Some time ago I read scary reports about "stressed teenagers" blaming Mum. This was in *The Sunday Times* which informed us that "new research shows that 40% of teenagers blame their busy working mothers for their problems".

Frankly, I find this staggering. Where were the other 60%, for heaven's sake? Asleep, or something? If modern teenagers are too apathetic to haul themselves out of bed and tick the box saying "Blame Mum", I think we have real cause for concern. As far as I can make out, we mothers, working or (pah!) not, are upholding our end of the bargain by being totally sad, like really embarrassing, and generally ruining our children's lives. You'd think the least they could do is blame us.

Personally, I can't function properly without guilt. It is a mother's lot. Do you go out to work? Neglecting your child! GUILTY! Do you stay at home with the kids? Wasting your education! GUILTY! Are you juggling career and children? Failing at both! GUILTY! And on top of that, for the Evangelical Christian mother – are you failing to demonstrate that the redeeming work of Christ "breaks the power of cancelled sin" by feeling guilty? HAH! GUILTY!

Yes, guilt is our medium, and if we are forced to operate in a different mode – feeling basically OK about ourselves, say – we start to get worried. The good news here is that it is but a short step from feeling worried about nothing to feeling guilty about it.

Church Sporting Tip of the Week

When you are wearing vestments of any kind, take care when kneeling. Do not step on the hem of your robes or you will do a nosedive when you attempt to stand up. Points will be deducted at major sporting fixtures (eg ordinations) from candidates who trip in this manner.

Chapter 5

FOOTBALL?

Feast of St Leger, patron of horse racing, 11 September

Extreme Sport

In early 2003, a VIK was lucky enough to have extended study leave, which we spent as a family in New Zealand. Those of you who have seen the three-part promotional tourist video of the country[6] will know how spectacular the landscape is. There are many vantage points from which to admire the scenery. I *believe* it is possible to enjoy it sitting quietly in a deckchair with a nice glass of New Zealand Sauvignon Blanc, but I'd have to say there is a great deal of pressure on you to enjoy it while being dropped headfirst down from a great height, or catapulted violently over rapids wondering if you will ever see your dear children again. Yes, New Zealand is the birthplace of extreme sport.

The Luge

One of the first things we did on arriving in Queenstown was to take the gondola ride up the steep mountainside to the top, where we got those breathtaking, staggering (insert wild adjective of choice), panoramic views out across Lake Wakatipu and the Remarkables, a range of mountains that are, well, remarkable. Included in the ticket price was a ride on the luge. For once this wasn't as scary as the image

---

6. Popularly known as *The Lord of the Rings*.

25

it conjured up (of sliding down an Alp on a tea tray dressed in Lycra. Lycra is such a punishing fabric for the mature figure when combined with a bumpy track, I always think). Instead we took a chairlift even higher and raced down some steep twisty slopes on little toboggan-like carts with steering and brakes. You can see at once that this doesn't count as an extreme sport. Your basic rule of thumb is: if it has steering and brakes and doesn't detach your retinas, it's not an extreme sport.

Jetboating

Given all the white-knuckle options available, I'm afraid we chose another nancyboy option in extreme sporting terms. Instead of whitewater rafting, or naked freefall kayaking (OK, I made that one up), we took a jetboat ride out across Lake Wakatipu and up the Shotover River. We donned life-jackets and ankle-length hooded raincoats (perfect for Nazgul impressions), clambered aboard and were cheerily greeted by our pilot, who seemed reassuringly competent in a "your retinas are safe with me" kind of a way. "You might like to hold on to the hand rails and brace your feet on the foot rests," he suggested, "as it may get a bit bumpy." Later I understood that this was an example of the dry Kiwi understatement.

With a roar of engines we were off, the hull thumping on the waves and the whole boat skidding about like a wet hard-boiled egg round a plate. Spray was smashed across us and the wind snatched our breath until it was all we could do to gasp, "Looks like I picked the wrong morning to wash my hair!" The faster we went, the "bumpier" it got. ("Looks like I picked the wrong morning to eat breakfast!")

I can't help feeling there was a bit of mild tourist-baiting going on, with the boat hurtling at high speed towards obstacles before veering away in the last nanosecond and missing them by a hairsbreadth. The only method of stopping appeared to be an abrupt 180-degree turn which sent another arc of spray across the passengers. After about the third of these our pilot looked round at us bedraggled landlubbers and observed in some surprise, "Another wet one, huh?" We nodded weakly. "Good job you're wearing those raincoats," he remarked guilelessly.

It struck me that lakes serve a different purpose over there. In our own English Lake District they are for wandering lonely as a cloud, hiking, or perhaps doing a spot of watercolour painting. A host of golden jetboats roaring across Windermere would rather disrupt the vacant or pensive mood.

Extreme Sport and The Church of England

Let it not be said that we Anglicans are incapable of relishing a challenge. We enjoy an adrenalin rush as much as the next chap. In this volume we will be encountering some of the more popular branches of Extreme Anglicanism, and exploring their appeal.

Chapter 6
FOOTBALL 5

Extreme Anglicanism

Door-to-Door Collecting

Door-to-door collecting is something I never do. But this is OK. As in every sport, the role of the spectator is not to be dismissed. For those who are keen door-to-door collectors, it is the white-knuckle element that appeals, that tremendous endorphin surge that comes of not knowing what lies behind the door you have just knocked on.

A VIK noticed an upturn in spontaneous generosity a couple of years ago as he went around door-to-door collecting for Christian Aid. Whether this was linked in any way with his new minimalist hairstyle,[7] or that of his fellow collector,[8] we may never discover. Certainly, if I found a couple of bald bruisers on my doorstep, I might not hear the polite "Good evening, we're from St Paul's" over the unspoken subtext: "Nice porch, shame if anything happened to it." Still, on one doorstep they found themselves wrong-footed. A guy came to the door stark naked and announced, "I'm sorry – I'm in the middle of something."

Becoming a Bishop

There are few Anglican sports more physically and emotionally demanding than that of being a bishop. People occasionally complain

---

7. ie, Scary bald bloke.
8. See above, n7.

29

about bishops' salaries being so much higher than that of the humble parson. The extra cash isn't so that bishops can sit around on silk hassocks smoking fat cigars and knocking back chalicefuls of *vino sacro*. No, it is danger money.

Personal Sporting Testimony

My Own Episcopal Calling

Sometimes I get restless in my role as vicar's wife. Ruling the tea urn can only go so far towards fulfilling my craving for phenomenal cosmic power. My ambition was sharpened a while back when I spotted an advert: "Vacancy in the See of Hereford!" Could this be a call? God moves in mysterious ways, and none more mysterious than the classified ads in the church press. Why, that is how we ended up at our present post. I can still remember the evening, over six years ago now, when a VIK came in and announced he was sending off for details of a job he'd seen advertised. "Where is it?" I asked. "Walsall," he replied. And I, in my open-hearted and faith-filled way, said, "There's *no way* I'm going to the West Midlands."[9]

But to return to my main topic, my call to be Bishop of Somewhere. In my ignorance of canon law I hadn't realised that being a lay person was no obstacle. Thomas Becket wasn't a priest when he was appointed Archbishop of Canterbury. I was making the basic error of seeing deacon and priest as hoops you have to jump through before you get a purple shirt. It turns out you can simply be ordained before you are consecrated: deacon, priest, then straight to bishop, in a kind of three-for-the-price-of-one deal. This is so that your ministry will be *catholic* and *inclusive*.

In theory, a total lack of experience of leading services, preaching, baptising, putting out chairs, fobbing people off with sandwiches when they really want the train fare to Glasgow – in short, all the things which go to make up ordained ministry – is no bar to becoming a bishop. Unless you make the fundamental blunder of

---

9. This is despite having been born in Stourport, I might add. "Ah, yow'm one of us," I was told when that piece of information was leaked. And proud of it, I can now say.

possessing X chromosomes, that is. If you are a woman you can't be a bishop, even if you've had years of parish experience and oodles of responsibility. This is because your ministry would not be *catholic* and *inclusive* – of bigots, is the phrase which springs unbidden to mind. No, I renounce that unhelpful thought as unworthy of a bishop.

I have a theory about bishop adverts, though. It's a means of weeding out those who are self-promoting. Don't apply. Wait to be asked.

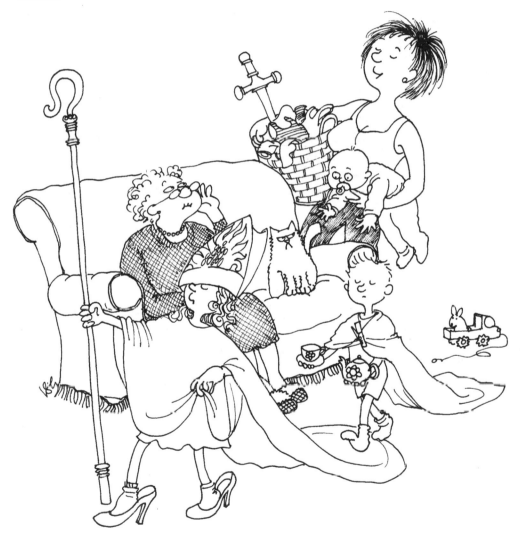

"It's a miracle play, Granny."

Chapter 7
FOOTBALL 6

Croquet Sunday
being the All England Handicap Final

Extreme Everyday Sport

All of Life is Sport. Therefore some normal everyday activities qualify as extreme sport, in my opinion. Blackwater rafters may sneer, but these are dangerous pastimes nonetheless.

Eating Junk Food

Eating rubbish is one of the easiest ways of dicing with death. Bungee-jumping and skydiving are OK in their way, but they take some organising. How much simpler to shovel in the fatty sugary food while larding about on the sofa. This may not sound particularly white-knuckle, but believe me, it's got the government pretty jumpy, not to mention the big food companies. In 2003 Kraft was leading the way in "making its snacks healthier to ward off lawsuits from consumers". Food, according to the media, was "the new tobacco".

If food is indeed the new tobacco, we may find the whole front half of our cereal packets will be obscured by block capitals saying, "EATING TRASH KILLS". One of the problems with the big threatening health warnings, however, is that we already *know* what's bad for us. Young people read the words "Smoking Kills", but their powers of observation tell them that it doesn't kill you instantly. It's not like saying, "Blowing your head off with a shotgun kills." The links between cause and effect are not immediate enough to override the pleasure of the moment.

Extreme Anglicanism

Laundry

Many people regard laundry as a mundane business. Not so in the vicarage. In ordinary homes it can be annoying if you accidentally get a red sock in with the white load, but lay people know nothing of that heart-stopping moment of opening the machine door and discovering that you've dyed a cassock alb puce.

Our washing machine broke a while ago and had to be repaired. This was after a week of me sending out the vicar's knickers to various trusted parishioners to launder. It turns out there was a rogue elastic band stuck in the pump. This strikes me as a bit of a design fault, but the engineer sternly suggested I be careful in future to check all garment pockets before loading the machine. This is all very well, but has he ever counted the number of pockets on the average youth trouser? You could get up Everest without a backpack or Sherpa in a pair of those. My older son even has some with pockets on the *knees*. What is he supposed to put in there? Polyester wadding, so he can do a goal-scoring victory slide across the playground without hurting himself?

Sport of the Week – Expectorating

As a general rule I don't advocate spitting as a pastime, but there are exceptions, one of them being the desperate effort to keep children amused in the hour before a wedding service. I'm not talking about vulgar flobbing, so much as the finely honed competitive cherry-stone projection that a vicar, for example, might appropriately indulge in with his sons. There are two styles: the basic tongue flick, or the bilabial plosive (or "raspberry") method. Either may be accompanied by the tennis serve grunt. Older competitors may attempt the nectarine-stone event, but only if there is someone around who can do the Heimlich manoeuvre.

Chapter 8
FOOTBALL 7

Emotional Workout

Many people think of emotions as an impersonal force, like internal weather, perhaps, over which we have little control. But there are things we can work at here. We can practise the art of contentment, for example. And believe me, this can be as demanding as running uphill in January when you're overweight and the New Year's resolution is fading fast. We can also work on nurturing a good environment for emotional health. Which leads us to:

The Gentle Art of Cherishing

It came to me in a wedding a while ago that "cherish" is a lovely word. Isn't it nice that the couple promise not only to love but to *cherish* one another? It comes, as you will be aware, from the Old French *chérir*, from *cher*, meaning "dear". My mother is big on cherishing anyone she thinks might need it, and I try to follow her example. It involves things like baking people cakes, or doing their washing up, or sending them flowers. My rule of thumb is this: if it makes them crumple into tears, you've got it about right.[10]

The other things to cherish are hopes and ambitions and ideas. We may do this for other people as well as ourselves. My sons, for example, cherish the hope that I will never wear my embarrassing sunglasses in public again. They feel so strongly about this that I can see possibilities for the offending specs as a form of crowd control. In

---

10. NB This *excludes* things like Chinese burns and punches to the kidney.

marriage each partner will cherish the hope that the other will thrive and shine and become the person they were meant to be. Personally, I've never understood it when spouses run one another down. What are we saying here, people? "Hey, everybody, look at how stupid I am for marrying them!"

Martial Art of the Week

Dressing Children Smartly

Choice of wedding clothes is an area of tense negotiation in the vicarage. It can easily deteriorate into outright war. My starting position is this: I would rather my sons wore jeans and ratty trainers and smiled, than collar and tie and were in a foul temper all day. We then hope to meet somewhere between those two extremes. This involves going round every single shop in Walsall which sells Young Person shirts, trying to find styles that a) my older son will consent to wear and b) I am prepared to buy. Fortunately, the younger son is still of an age where he will wear anything I thrust at him, provided it's not pink, or his older brother tells him it's sad.

I still retain the upper hand, of course, not just because I wield the wallet, but because of my more advanced retailing skills. After an hour or so, I can force a purchase by saying, "So you're telling me you prefer the *first* one we saw? You're sure you want to go *all the way back* to British Home Stores to buy the first one? OK, come along then. It's only a mile away. I'll buy you an ice cream *after* we've bought it." And as a last resort I can always say, "You're having this one, or I'm putting the sunglasses on." "No, no, NOT the sunglasses, Mother!"

Biblical Sporting Hero of the Week

Jehu, patron of Boy Racers everywhere. He was renowned for driving his high-performance E-type chariot "very furiously".

"*And you think you've got problems?*"

Chapter 9
FOOTBALL 8

Billabong Sunday

A Note on Billabong Sunday

This festival celebrates the noble art of surfing, and the major festivities may be enjoyed at the National Surfing Championships at Newquay. Not all of us are able to make the pilgrimage down to Cornwall, or capable of standing upright on a surfboard when we get there. This does not mean that the day cannot be marked in ordinary parishes up and down the land. Many vestments catalogues now offer an extensive range of liturgical surf wear for the clergy. Suitable liturgies for Billabong Sunday may be downloaded from *Common Worship*. Here is an example:

> *Priest:* Dude!
> *Congregation:* **Dude!**
> *Priest:* I'm like, hey, peace be with you, dude.
> *Congregation:* **Yeah, with you too, awesome priest dude!**

Extreme Sport

The Australian Way

Just living quietly in an ordinary suburb of Sydney constitutes an extreme sport in my book. This is not to say Sydney is an unpleasant city. Far from it. I was lucky enough to stay there for a few days on our way back from New Zealand. I woke up one morning to the sound of kookaburras and currawongs singing in the bush. You will infer from this that a currawong is a kind of bird, but the wonderful thing about Australia is that I could invent any number of names and facts, and most of you would never know, any more than you have the faintest idea what the words of "Waltzing Matilda" mean. Billabong, currawong, wangdoodle. There is even a species of bird called "thickheads", according to my reference book.

I was able to look out of my window in Sydney directly at the bush. By "bush" I mean "native forest". I mention that in case you've always visualised the "merry little king of the bush" as a small bird in a shrub. This is how I always pictured it as a child when we sang the round at primary school. The other thing I'll just clarify is the bird's size. If you picture a mottled brown and cream kingfisher the size of a chicken, that's basically your kookaburra. Or rather, that's your *laughing* kookaburra. As opposed to your blue-winged kookaburra, which, unsurprisingly, has blue wings. They can also be distinguished by their different calls, according to the bird book I borrowed. The laughing kookaburra has a "loud chuckling laugh", whereas the blue-winged kookaburra's call is "extended maniacal laughter".

Unless that's just the sound of the poor ornithologist trekking through the bush and encountering a Sydney funnel-web spider. I think that a city having its very own lethal spider is a bit much. But that's Australia for you. There is an extravagance, a largesse about the place. Birmingham is a similar size to Sydney, but I can't imagine a Birmingham funnel-web spider, for instance. Well, I can, but even I wouldn't have come up with the idea of a spider which hides in its lair and flies out into your unsuspecting face like a coiled spring, sinking its venomous fangs into your flesh. According to a leaflet belonging to my hosts, entitled, "Australian SNAKES and other VENOMOUS CREATURES Decoder", the Sydney ("very aggressive and dangerous") funnel-web spider "can bite through a child's fingernail". And – you'll like this – the leaflet observes in passing that "the Northern Tree-Dwelling Funnel-Web is even more dangerous". It probably bungee-jumps onto your head and rips your scalp off as you pass underneath.

So if you are planning a bird-spotting trip in Australia, wear stout shoes, don't poke your finger in any holes, don a crash helmet and, above all, *stay indoors*.

Great Sporting Challenges of our Time – Cleaning the Shower

This is an annual event and usually coincides with the arrival of visitors. The trickiest aspect is rinsing off the cleaning product after you've scrubbed the walls and floor of the cubicle. How are you to rinse the inside of the door? Do you stand inside? Fully clothed? Stark naked? Or do you try and close the door, yet leave an arm inside to manipulate the shower head? Should you combine this event with the floor washing challenge? Or do you ring your guests and check whether they are short-sighted, in which case you won't need to clean the shower at all?

Chapter 10
FOOTBALL 9

Extreme Barbering

Barbering is not generally regarded as a sport these days. The traditional barber's pole, with its spiralling red stripe denoting freely flowing blood, is mere nostalgic trumpery. You don't expect to shed blood when you get your hair cut in the 21st century. But hairdressing can still be a bit of a pulse-raiser if it's done right.

The Skinhead Cut

There is something about being on the other side of the world which liberates you to try out new things. In the case of a VIK this meant shaving his head in our first few weeks in New Zealand. Messages of disapproval filtered through from the congregation back home – as soon as they were convinced that the email photo was for real, and not some clever digital prank by the curate. Our sons were not convinced by their clean-shaven father either, but settled down soon enough when we reminded them what happens in the Bible to little boys who shout "Baldy!" at their elders.

Head-shaving among men in their 40s is increasingly common. It is a kind of valiant pre-emptive strike by a man seeking to regain control. Personally, I've had a theory for a while about male hair loss. I think it could better be described as male hair *migration*. It starts to leave the forehead or the crown, but it makes its stealthy way elsewhere – to the man's chest, his nostrils, ears and, more alarmingly still, to the upper lip and chin of his female partner. That's my explanation of the sudden luxuriance of the female moustache once you hit 40.

Wouldn't it be in the interests of both parties to come to some kind of an agreement? I'm thinking about men who undergo hair transplants, having tiny plugs of their already sparse hair replanted on their bald patch. Wouldn't it be better for all concerned if *women* donated their unwanted follicles? No more waxing or electrolysis. I think there's some mileage in the idea.

The Great Indoors

Home Barbering

A good haircut is not cheap, but there are ways of economising. I found that buying a set of clippers and buzzing my sons' hair every month soon pays for my salon habit. It also solves any head louse problems. No more tedious fine-combing – just plough the suckers.

The position of family barber is a post of fearsome responsibility. A midwife I know once blithely zipped into her husband's hair without putting the guard on the clippers. There was nothing else for it but to shave the whole lot off. I'd like to go on record as saying that this is *not* why a VIK now sports a clean-shaven head. He did it himself of his own free will. And why not? People should be allowed to do as they please with their hair, provided their barnet is not a hazard near working machinery.

Great Sporting Challenges of our Time – Dealing with Nasal Hair

I have a theory that one of the most common 40th birthday presents for men – though nobody will admit this – is the nasal hair trimmer. It will be bought for him by his loving partner, and he will never use it. This is because men do not, by and large, spend enough time in front of the bathroom mirror examining themselves. The only time they study their reflections is when they are stuck in a traffic jam getting bored. After fiddling about with the radio and swapping lanes pointlessly a few times, they eventually run out of things to do and fall to studying themselves in the driver's mirror with a view to flossing their teeth with an old pay-and-display ticket.

"What's *that*? A *hair*?!" they cry in horror. Obviously, the nasal

"I'm back off home to Minsk — at least we got shouted at there!"

hair trimmer is at home in the bathroom cabinet, so they are obliged, with loud yips of pain, to try and pull the straggler out manually. The solution here is to keep the trimmer tucked behind the visor. Manufacturers should ensure their personal grooming devices are cigarette lighter compatible.

Chapter 11
FOOTBALL 10

Extreme Anglicanism

Dressing Up

There's not much point becoming an Anglican if you are allergic to fancy dress. Even if you find yourself a nice low church where the vicar wears a collar and tie, you will still have your sensibilities affronted at confirmations and ordinations, when grown men in frocks are the order of the day.

Personally, I'm partial to a bit of fancy dress, whether at parties or in the nave. Last year, however, a VIK and I decided we were not going to host our annual church garden party. I think this was the right decision, but I have to admit, it left a fancy dress-shaped hole in my life which ordinary parties cannot fill. Luckily, our next-door neighbours were having a 21st birthday party with a Wild West theme. "Fancy dress compulsory," said the invitation in the bracing and forthright way these secular types can get away with. Try telling Anglicans something's compulsory and they'll go off and join another church.

A quick rummage in the attic yielded some passable Mexican bandit outfits, and off we went. I thought I looked rather dashing, but I was taken aside early on by a fellow guest who whispered, "I hope you don't mind my saying so, but you've been a *leetle* heavy-handed with the make-up." This was from a six-foot-five transvestite with balloons down his cleavage. We had a girlie chat about false fingernails, which I pooh-poohed. I mean, how can you pick your nose wearing *them*? I wondered. He replied loftily that *he* had people to do that for him.

Sporting Tip of the Week

What Not to Wear on a Bucking Bronco

The highlight of the evening was undoubtedly the bucking bronco machine our neighbours had hired. Great fun for all the family, and for us, of course, it had the added benefit of propelling us over the fence home, saving us the walk. The basic rule is that you stay on as long as the guy operating it decides you're going to. If he is feeling merciful, you will last several minutes. The landing is soft – the steer is surrounded by a kind of inflatable bouncy castle crash mat. All it takes is a mad impulse, a good sense of balance and thighs of iron.[11]

A few words of warning, though. Drink enough for Dutch courage, but no more – especially if you are prone to motion sickness. Think through your underwear situation in advance. You cannot control your dismount. This is no place for thongs. Or balloons, come to think of it.

Sporting Rules and Regulations

Some governing bodies are very strict about such things as proper kit. Take Wimbledon, for example: players turning up in the wrong colour shirt will have to go off the court and get changed. Jeans and trainers will not be allowed on the golf course. Sometimes I feel, as I look about me, that in the more low-key sport of Life people are in desperate need of guidance and a firm hand. Things would be so much easier if some benevolent official body, the Department of Sartorial Wisdom, perhaps – not a couple of self-appointed bossyboots off the TV – told us what we were supposed to wear. When I'm democratically elected minister of this new department, I will immediately introduce some guidelines. They will be shouted through police loud hailers and from hovering helicopters at anyone found transgressing them in a public place:

1. Buy a bra that fits! (women)
2. Put the belly away! (everybody)

---

11. I think this has distinct potential as a tool for selecting new bishops.

3. Keep the thong below the waistband! (girls)
4. If it's thinning out, cut it short! (blokes)
5. Stay clear of working machinery in those trousers! (young people)
6. Trim your eyebrows! (bishops)

Chapter 12
FOOTBALL 11

Extreme Everyday Sport

House Buying

The more I see of the anguish of house buying in this country, the more grateful I am that I don't have to do it. I can't think of a single instance of the process going through smoothly. As far as I can see, until you have actually got the keys to your new house, you have to be prepared for the whole thing to fall through. What I can't understand is why the whole business has to be so hideously complex, so riddled with pitfalls and last minute hitches. People have been buying and selling houses for generations. Why is the system still so inefficient?

The other thing I can't really understand is why there aren't instances of conveyancing rage all the time. I think I speak for everyone who isn't actually a solicitor when I wonder why more people aren't marching into the offices of Cockup & Dawdle brandishing a meat cleaver?[12]

But I daresay the whole thing looks different from behind the desk of a busy solicitor. It is one thing to deal efficiently with a single house sale, another to run 50 odd sales concurrently, even if that is precisely what you are being paid to do. Part of the problem lies in the collision of different perspectives. The house buyer is only buying one house. It is the focus of all their hopes and anxieties and plans. A house is much, much more than just a roof over your head. People

---

12. Probably because the meat cleaver is already packed in a crate labelled "Kitchen" underneath six other crates waiting for the move.

trying to buy a house often say to me, "I'm trying not to set my heart on it." The problem with this is that it's not much fun buying somewhere if you *haven't* fallen in love with it. At the very least we like to have the housing equivalent of a mild crush. I suppose solicitors are a kind of marriage broker. Not many of their clients are coolly entering a marriage of convenience.

Health and Diet

How to Get Fat

I was talking to a beautiful young African woman the other day. She was tall and had what all women recognise as one of those "I hate you" figures. You know, around size 10, only with curves. It was made all the more galling by the fact that she had a fifteen-month-old baby. This is the stage when most mothers are wondering how come all that weight hasn't just dropped off, like everyone promised it would when you stopped breastfeeding.

And yet this young woman was not happy with her body. Isn't that *so* predictable? you groan. Yes, she wants to be a size 18. She has always been skinny and she hates it. I told her she was the opposite of almost every woman in England. Indeed, at least two Englishwomen stepped up straightaway, clutching their midriff flab and volunteering, "Here, have some of mine!" I have vulgar friends. Generous, but vulgar.[13]

My new African friend said to me despairingly, "I eat lots of fatty food!" "What about sugar?" I asked, mindful of the Wisdom of Atkins. "Lots!" she replied. "And I don't do any exercise!" Hmm. I racked my brain. I like to be helpful, and there is a small and secret part of every Western woman who doesn't *mind* making other people fatter, especially if they are young and gorgeous.

I think the solution must be counterintuitive. The best way of gaining weight is to try and lose it. Put yourself on a rigorously low fat calorie-controlled diet, then cave in after two days and go on a junk food binge. It seems to be working for most people.

---

13. And because they might conceivably read this, I will confess straightaway that one of them wasn't a friend at all. It was me.

Biblical Sport of the Week

Millstone-hurling

This is an Old Testament sport, usually reserved for women. The player stands on a high parapet of a city wall and, taking careful aim, hurls her millstone at her opponent. The objective is to dash his brains out.

Warning: owing to large parts, this game is not suitable for under threes.

Chapter 13
FOOTBALL 12

Performance-Enhancing Substances

Testosterone

Did you know that your ring finger has more testosterone receptors than your other fingers? Research shows that the longer a man's ring finger, the more exposed he was to testosterone in the womb, and the more pre-birth testosterone, the more rugged and macho the grown man.

I'd have to say that here in the vicarage not all of us were convinced by the argument when we read it in our paper. Here is a verbatim record of the commentary made by my older son, in a drolly bored voice, as he read the article: "Oh dear. My ring finger is shorter than my index finger. My willy is fake. How foolish of me to think I was boy all these years. And look, I am going to die of breast cancer."

A VIK was similarly unfazed by his ring finger inadequacies. Indeed, it was the present author who won the testosterone finger test in this house. This accounts for my craggy good looks and moustache. It also means (you may choose) I am a gay man, a lesbian, that I produce more than average amounts of sperm, am at risk from heart disease or am more likely to suffer from autism, dyslexia and left-handedness.

Extreme Sport

Camping

Once in a while my menfolk go off camping in a male-bonding, Iron John kind of way. I daresay they light fires by rubbing their ring fingers together so that they can feast on the tinned spaghetti hoops they hunted down in the supermarket before they set off. The task is usually something like this: to camp overnight in a field among wild beasts, then climb Snowdon the following morning. During the camping part of the ritual, the son's task is to sit bolt upright at fifteen-minute intervals throughout the night and demand in fearful tones, "What was that?" The father's job is to grunt sleepily and mutter something about sheep.

It is well-recognised here in the vicarage that there's no point calling "Dad!" if you've had a bad dream. If he can be roused at all, the most he will do is administer a clumsy pat and say, "Go back to sleep." I, on the other hand, have been known to sing songs, talk reassuringly for hours on end and even draw a mongoose at 3am to ward off the snakes under the bed. But transfer the scene to canvas under the elements and everything changes. Suddenly Mum is no use. The normal boundaries (which four walls place upon her imagination) vanish. "What was *that*?!" "I don't know! Maybe it's a feral mink grown to monstrous proportions after a radiation leak from a nearby power plant and bearing a grudge against humans utilising animal products. Oh no! Our hiking boots are leather! We're done for!"

The second part of the challenge, climbing Snowdon, may also find out the limits of a mother's usefulness. Primed as we are to nurture and protect our little ones, we may respond a little too early to their hints about bad weather, steepness, blisters, feet worn down to bleeding stumps and so on, and say, "Well, don't worry. It doesn't matter. You don't have to do it." What a boy really requires is his dad to say bracing things like, "You're doing really well, not far now, I'm sure your feet will grow back etc" and coax him to the summit.

Great Sporting Challenges of our Time — Putting the Bin out

This is only a minor physical challenge. There is, however, something about the act of putting out the bin that challenges our normal mental processes, and possibly the nature of reality itself. The issue is this: every single adult member of any household is always utterly convinced that he or she is *the only one who ever puts the bin out.*

"You know what men are like with the remote control. I haven't had to lift a finger since I bought that auto-bin."

Chapter 19

FOOTBALL 13

Synchro-Sunday
being The Synchronised Swimming
National Championships

Extreme Anglicanism

Liturgical Synchronised Swimming

This is a relatively new event to Anglicanism, having grown out of modern liturgical dance, which it very much resembles. The main differences are the addition of nose clips, and the abandoning of loose nylon kaftans and big swirly flags. It is on such occasions as baptisms at public swimming baths that liturgical synchro-swimming comes into its own.

Extreme Sport

Swimming with Dolphins

This is not as extreme as swimming with piranhas, but I reckon we can make a case for swimming with dolphins as being an extreme-ish sport. We were lucky enough to go swimming with dolphins just south of Christchurch while we were in New Zealand. I'd imagined that this would take place in some sort of swimming pool, with an attendant saying, "And this is Bubbles. Come and introduce yourself to the nice people, Bubbles!", whereupon Bubbles would bob up obligingly to be stroked before doing a couple of somersaults, catching a fish in mid-air, and swimming off again.

Wrong. These were wild dolphins and this meant taking a boat out to sea and jumping off into icy water too deep to touch the bottom, while wearing a wet suit which made you look fat and tipped you face downwards when you were least expecting it, and waiting for the dolphins to appear. And they did. With no warning, there they were sliding past, or arching through the water right through the middle of the group. Once, I had my face in the water and saw one close enough to touch and could hear its strange clicking sound. But they were elusive. You barely had time to gasp – not advisable with a snorkel in your mouth – and they were off. I so wanted them to come up face to face and look at me, but they never did. But perhaps they were mourning, "We click to them, but they never reply!"

Why do they like to come and play among these strange rubber-clad bobbing lumps of tourist, I wonder? I'm glad they do. These were Hector's dolphins, small, and travelling in a small pod. I gather that Dusky dolphins, which you can also swim with in New Zealand, are a slightly different proposition. They are larger, and travel in groups of between 40 and – wait for it – 800. I'd think twice before calling them Bubbles, if I were you.

Extreme Anglicanism

Planning your Own Funeral

Some time ago a VIK suddenly asked me if I'd chosen my funeral hymns. On reflection, I decided there was nothing sinister to be read into this. It isn't in the same category as seeing your spouse fiddling around suspiciously under the car bonnet, then waving you off on a long journey with the words, "Drive safely! Oh, did I mention I've just insured your life for half a million pounds?"

No, the reason he posed this question was because we were listening to Edith Piaf's "*Je ne regrette rien*", a song which was played at the funeral of a friend of ours a few years ago. Our sons asked what the words meant and a VIK explained. "Would you have it at your funeral, Mum?" I was asked. I told them that in all conscience, I couldn't. There was a dodgy perm in late 1983 which I regret deeply.

So what would I choose instead? I suppose it would be a toss up between Handel's "The trumpet shall sound" and Nina Simone's "Feeling good". But why choose? I'll have both. It's my funeral, after all. I'll have what I jolly well want. Unfortunately, though, I won't be in a strong position to argue. When it comes to it, I can't stop them having "Ding dong, the witch is dead"!

Chapter 15
FOOTBALL 19

Bloodsports

Every so often I feel the need to get out into the countryside. Town life offers many advantages: pound shops, the opportunity to go merrymaking in your underwear and fall on your face drunk, handily situated Accident & Emergency departments, free pizza delivery and museums. These benefits go a long way towards consoling me for the lack of open green spaces, but my heart is in the country.

Sort of. I grew up in a slightly odd environment where heavy industry and rural life lived cheek by jowl. There was one place in our village where you could stand and admire the view of the local windmill in its cornfield against a backdrop of the cement works. Our car had what my father always described as a reinforced concrete finish from the factory dust that settled on it. He used to clean it with steel wool. You will infer from this that we didn't have either a garage or a smart motor. In fact, we had a Wartburg, an East German car which required you to add two-stroke oil to the petrol. This was fun, especially when my older sister could drive and was filling the tank. Any bloke watching would bellow and wave his hands frantically: No, no, you daft bird!

Anyway, our village was not posh rural, by any stretch of the imagination, but even we had our Boxing Day Meet. Strictly speaking, it was in the next village, which was a little classier than ours. I can remember seeing the hunters gather opposite the village green with their red coats which they called pink, and their white horses they called grey. It had a certain olde worlde charm, full of arcane terminology and ritual.

If your heart is even sort of in the country, you will naturally have a view about fox hunting. This is why I found it pretty distressing to see the rough treatment dished out to the pro-hunt protesters a while ago. Town life has obviously turned me into a bit of a softie. It took me several minutes to see past all those battered bloodstained faces on our TV screens and remind myself that the protesters actually *enjoy* it. The other thing we bleeding heart liberals must bear in mind is that without pro-hunt demonstrations of this kind there are going to be a lot of redundant riot police who will have to be put down. Nobody wants *that*.

Emotional Workout – Taming the Wild Beast Within

Here I'd like to commend my own bloodsport of preference: judo. One of the important things judo teaches is how to handle physical strength in a controlled way. And this, too, is one of the important things fathers should teach their sons. That is what's going on when dads and sons play-fight. In the past in our house it invariably ended in tears, but this is all part of the process. It is teaching boys how to deal with strong emotion without lashing out. While they are still learning, any lashing out can be safely contained by Dad.

Martial Art of the Week – Judo

Gender and Judo

There is an arcane world of gender etiquette in martial arts. Normally, a large bloke does not use violence on a woman. That would be against the spirit of judo, as well as unchivalrous. But at the same time, a bloke cannot actually permit a woman to win, as he would lose face and be taunted by all the other blokes on the mat.

No, a bloke might sportingly *allow* a woman to strangle him, for example, especially if he is coaching her in the dark arts of semi-legal tactics. In fact, some seem to take great pleasure in this, going blue in the face and choking out the words, "That's working – it's coming on now!" before blacking out, coming to again, retching and coughing, and giving you a cheery thumbs up.

I think blokes particularly enjoy coaching women, because they are secure in the knowledge that they can always win by brute force if an emergency threat to male pride arises. So if I ever get roughed up, I take it as a sign that I'm doing well enough to be causing them problems.

Useful Gadget of the Week

A Baptist minister I know rang me a while back to say he'd seen an "electric home shredder" for sale in a local shop. Handy for those who don't have small children to do it for them.

Chapter 16
FOOTBALL 15

Feast of the Blessed Jonny Wilkinson, 22 November

The Great Indoors – White-Knuckle Internet Surfing

Ah, the Final Judgement and the world of computers! What a rich seam for the preacher to mine. One of my theories of life is that nothing is ever wasted in the vicarage. It can either be sent to a charity shop, used as a sermon illustration, or made into soup. This is why, in a spirit of usefulness, I am now about to expose my own weakness and folly to you in order to provide material for pious reflection.

Yes, I admit it. My computer got a very nasty virus a while ago. Two quick pieces of computing advice here for free: a) make sure your anti-virus is up to date and b) don't let your children download things onto your computer.[14] The good news is that there is a special destination for the writers of computer viruses. It was revealed to me in a vision. They will be locked in a small room in the afterlife and not let out until they have written a programme that de-activates original sin and undoes its effects on human history. The rest of us get to sit drinking cappuccinos on the Left Bank of the River of Life under the giant mimosa trees.

---

14. Always make sure they use another adult's machine instead.

Extreme Parenting

Pocket Money

They are all con merchants, these children. They are forever claiming you don't give them enough pocket money, and that everyone else in their class gets more than them. Mostly we parents have to accept this as part of the So Not Fair package, which normally includes everyone else

- being allowed to stay up till midnight on schooldays
- getting to watch 18 films
- going to Alton Towers with 20 mates for their birthday treat

But a survey by the Halifax Bank has put a stop to that pocket money gripe, at least. Far from being hard done by, pocket money "has increased 23 times faster than prices in general over the past year". I knew that would shock you. No wonder we have inflation. It's all very well us grown-ups making do with tiny pay increases when our good work and restraint is undermined by fat cat seven-year-olds earning 460% more than their predecessors in the 1980s.

I don't know what it is about pocket money, but I can never seem to get a grip on it. It reminds me of royalty statements, which appear to show that you have sold lots and lots of books, but for some reason that remains obscure, the publisher never actually owes you any money. Pocket money is equally complex. You are always dishing out cash, but at any given moment you always owe your child £35. And that's taking into account the times you raid their piggy bank to pay the milk bill.

Chapter 17
FOOTBALL 16

Health and Diet

The Tyranny of Convenience

When I was growing up, the spectre of rationing still peered over adult shoulders. You couldn't flick a pea across the room without grown-ups gasping, "That could have been the basis of a nutritious meal for 16 people!" and "Wilful waste makes woeful want!"

My children are growing up not knowing what food shortage is – well, unless they mean we've run out of crisps *again*. There is always food in the house. And usually it includes something they actually want to eat. They are allowed to help themselves. Within certain fair and rational limits, of course, based on how close it is to a meal, and what mood I'm in. When I think back to my early years, there really wasn't much worth pinching from our pantry. Raisins, perhaps, or jam. Cake and biscuits were always accounted for, and likely to be missed. There were times when we were so desperate we had to make our own candy floss by dipping cotton wool in the golden syrup tin.

Young people today, eh? Don't know they're born. There are moments when I feel guilty for allowing my children to graze, but at least they realise that meals can be constructed from individual fresh components, meat, vegetables and the like, not just stuck in the microwave and tipped onto a plate (if you're feeling dainty). The trouble is we're suckers for convenience these days. Convenient food, convenient car trips everywhere. And even convenient exercise gadgets that you can strap on to wobble your cellulite into submission while you sit on the sofa watching TV with a bag of kettle chips. No,

I admit that's a ludicrous idea. Nobody would be that self-deluding. You can't *hear* the TV if you're eating kettle chips.

I'm beginning to glimpse a vision of myself in old age. "The trouble with our society," I'll be saying as I buttonhole you in the doctor's waiting room, "is that people expect something for nothing. Results with no effort. Here, look at my scar. I've had half my stomach out. No discipline, that's what's wrong with the youngsters these days. I'm 97, you know."

By some oversight, I was not asked to sit on the Commons Health Select Committee on obesity. But I think this is the heart of the problem: we're being encouraged the whole time to think everything we want ought to be a conveniently available commodity, buy now, pay later, because we're worth it. If slenderness isn't offered on those terms, well, we want to know why not.

Spiritual Health

In these days of declining church attendance, the spiritual health of our congregations is something we need to take seriously. Old much-loved patterns may have to be jettisoned. We may need to adapt to survive. One of the current favourite new models of church life is "cell church". Here's a confession of personal stupidity – until recently I had never stopped to think what "cell" church meant. I suppose I was treating it a bit like one of those words you see written down, but have never actually heard anyone say, and consequently don't know how to pronounce. Or else you find out one day you've been mentally mispronouncing it for decades, like my younger sister with "wad unit", which was how she thought you said "whodunit".

But cell churches – the image I'd had in mind was that of a prison cell. This made sense to me. Sentenced for life to being locked in a small group! Imagine my relief at learning that *biological* cell was what other people had in mind. Different types of living cell, all with their different functions, but all sharing in the whole. A kind of celebration of diversity. As in, *I* am a brain cell, *you* are an appendix cell, but that's OK because we both have our part to play.

The Healthy Church – True Inclusivity

It's sometimes unfortunate that the "D" and the "F" keys are next to one another on a computer keyboard – as a VIK realised when he accidentally typed, "A joint service with the Church Among Dead People". That would be a reference to the communion of saints, I imagine.

Chapter 18
FOOTBALL 17

Extreme Everyday Sport

Shopping; Sub-Event: Christmas Shopping

This is very much a national sport, rather like self-deprecating irony and talking about the weather. The key thing here, I think, is that those of us with expertise and experience need to share that with those new to the sport, or lacking in confidence. This is why I am including a Christmas Shopping guide in this volume. I shall follow what I see to be the pattern set up by the colour supplements and divide my lists between various imagined age groups or personality types.

The mum in leather trousers

The leather trousers say, "Hey, I may be a mum who has just turned 40, but I'm still one foxy lady!" To affirm her in her new selfhood, why not pay for her to have her *belly-button pierced*, or a *small tattoo* done? She will also appreciate a *trip to a health spa*, a *bottle of champagne* and a large box of very classy *Belgian chocolates* to consume while watching her new *Pilates video*.

Trendy vicar (male)

He will probably be having a bit of a mid-life crisis, experimenting with a "two can play at that game!" approach to hair loss by having his head shaved. He might like a smart new *electric razor* and some expensive (yet not too gay) *moisturiser* to soothe his scalp. Now might also be the time for *linen suits, black cashmere polo necks* and a pair of sharp little *frameless specs* that say, "So I can no longer read the pew sheet without them even at arm's length, but you know what? I'm cool with that." This is also a good moment to buy him that *Lynnard Skynnard CD*, so he can drive along with the sunroof open listening to "Free Bird" and dreaming dreams.

Trendy vicar (female)

(See above, The mum in leather trousers. NB The small tattoo should be Celtic, and below the dog collar line.)

Trendy bishop

Only kidding.

Eight-year-old boy

I won't waste time by making suggestions. Simply give him an Argos catalogue and a pen (during a boring service, perhaps) and ask him to put a star by what he wants.

Eleven-year-old boy

Repeat the above exercise, substituting a GAME catalogue for the Argos one. He might also appreciate a can of *body spray*, so that he can experiment in preparation for his teen years by a) neglecting to use it, or b) spraying on the entire can in one go as a shower substitute.

For the children of people who have annoyed you

There is plenty of scope here. Try one of those *kung fu hamsters*, a *necklace-making kit* with a trillion small beads, a *remote control whoopee cushion*, *stink bombs*, or anything which requires hours of adult supervision while being assembled or operated. And don't forget the old standby, the *chemistry set*.

"*I like to see the young 'uns enjoying themselves.*"

Girls (junior school age)

This is easy. Go to your nearest Claire's Accessories, shut your eyes and randomly select articles up to the value of £5.

For the person who has got everything

Why not send a begging letter?

Chapter 19
FOOTBALL 18

Mental Workout

Maths

With tedious monotony our papers report on sliding standards and exam marking scandals of one kind or another. I remember reading an article about maths, once, approaching it with the kind of grisly fascination I might feel when reading a report on testicular disorders – deeply tragic, but not something I'm likely ever to suffer from. I said goodbye to maths in 1978, and apart from my annual tussle with the tax return, I've never have to do anything remotely arithmetical since.

The article was revealing that the standard of maths was so woeful this year that the C grade pass mark had to be dropped from 50% to 42% – that's a staggering 28% (or two-thirds), which, I'm sure you'll agree, is a genuine cause for concern. In my day there was no absolute fixed marking system. It was all done by percentages. If you were in the top x% you got an A. This was not entirely fair, of course. If you happened to be in a year full of nerdy little maths anoraks, you ended up with a lower grade. It also meant that there was no objective way of demonstrating whether national standards were going up or down. With the new system we can all tell. The standards are going up, tra la! Each year more students are gaining the A* to C grades they need to prove that the new system is better than the old one and the government is right to interfere and impose all this league-table-and-target cobblers on the educational system.[15]

---

15. Sorry, that sentence *should* have read, "...the A* to C grades they need to go on to take A-levels".

None of this stuff about objective measures of standards applies, naturally, if the exam boards go about dropping the pass mark. Anyone with an ounce (that's 7.5kg) of mathematical instinct can tell that once this starts happening we are basically back to the old system of grading, in which nobody can know anything objectively from the results – apart from the fact that the nerdy little anoraks will still always come top in maths.[16]

Natural Sporting Ability

My own theory is that maths, like many other sporting abilities, cannot be taught. It's innate. All teachers can do is *uncover* it in their pupils. There will always be perfectly intelligent adults who react to the simplest mathematical formula as if it were an ancient Urdu text. It rears up in their horrified faces like a vast unyielding cliff face on which their mind will never be able to gain any purchase, and off which their despairing scream will echo into silence. Keep dropping those pass marks, I say.

Important Sporting Equipment

Pants

I've never really understood why "pants" should have become a youth synonym for "bad" (that's "bad" in the grown-up sense, not "bad" meaning "good", or "wicked", ie "good"). I'm beginning to fear that there's a whole hinterland to the pants concept about which I know nothing. Why, for instance, did the TK Maxx receipt a VIK was given when he last bought underpants say, "Male furnishings"? Because blokes would be embarrassed if anyone picked up the receipt and read the word "pants"? Well, obviously if it said, "Silk posing pouch, XXS", that would be a bit blush-making, but *pants*? If "pants" are so problematical, why not say "male clothing"? What's this "furnishing" nonsense? Is it by way of an indirect boast? Hey, ladies, we chaps are so macho we require upholstering!

---

16. Unless I am very much mistaken, Pythagoras' theorem states that this remains constant, regardless of variations in the exam system.

MALE FURNISHINGS DEPARTMENT

STRETCH COVERINGS
REMOVABLE COVERINGS

BOLSTERS

EGO BOLSTERS

DRAPES

PROTECTIVE SPRAYS

LEATHER SEATINGS

WIPECLEAN COATINGS

DRIP-DRY COATINGS

TRIMMINGS

COD PIECES
ANTI-MASSACRES

"Right, boys, where would you like to start?"

Chapter 20
FOOTBALL 19

Culinary Sport

Winebuffery

Every now and then our Sunday papers offer us guides to wine. I feel there is an urgent need for an Evangelical Christian version, too. I offer this, not out of any wine expertise of my own, but out of a recognition that we really ought to have our own equivalent, just in case. Just in case of what, I'm not sure. In case we are accidentally seduced into worldliness of some kind, I imagine. This is why we have Christian novels and music and pencil sharpeners, after all. It's a dangerous world out there. If you wish to engage in the challenging sport of extreme wine-tasting, you will need help.

How to choose a white wine

Girlie method: Look for section saying "White". Pick up bottle at random. Examine the label. Is it pretty? Does it have nice lettering? If it's expensive, does that mean it will be nice? Dither for ten minutes, weeping at the complexity of it all, then choose a bottle with a rococo cherub on. (Or if you are under male headship, get your husband to do this for you).

Bloke method: Go straight to fridge and check if the Chardonnay is cold/under £4. Dither for three nanoseconds and buy Stella instead.

How to choose a red wine

Girlie method: Think: am I wearing pale colours? Do I have a cream sofa? Is this a dry-cleaning bill waiting to happen? Go to "White" section and buy warm Chardonnay.

Bloke method: Stand in "Red" section doing complex calculations to discover whether it would be cheaper to buy three bottles or one box. Notice that the Merlot is three for two. Re-do calculations. Go to fridge and buy Stella.

Communion wine

This is generally fortified wine, so that it doesn't turn into vinegar between Sunday services. There is no precedent in the Scriptures for turning vinegar back into wine. Neither is there one for turning QC ruby port into *vino sacro*, although this doesn't stop a VIK praying (so far unsuccessfully) that it will happen.

What does the Bible tell us about wine?

- it maketh glad the heart of man
- it getteth you drunk

The distance between the two is not as long a journey as one might think. They tell me. Our Lord himself turned water into wine. A VIK once calculated how much wine must have been involved and came up with a figure of something like an extra six bottles per guest.

Great Sporting Challenges of our Time

Extreme Baking

What many of us are seeking in the world of competitive baking is something to make for the church fête which isn't some kind of Nigella Lawson tribute. This idea came to me in the food hall of Birmingham's new Selfridges, where I was drawn to a stand where everyone wore expressions of acute disgust. I found myself viewing a stand devoted to insects and bugs as food. Tequila worms, giant hornets in honey, dried moths, ants in white chocolate – all at hugely inflated prices.[17]

So here's a handy church fête recipe for you:

Chocolate-covered insects

Ingredients:
    1 block fairly traded chocolate
    50g insects (eg ants, clothes moths, silver fish)[18]

Method: Melt chocolate and stir in insects. Spoon into fancy paper cases and refrigerate. (*Chef's hint:* it's always worth using a *really good* chocolate, or it won't taste nice.)

---

17. Contrary to popular belief, this is not the stock Brummie response to fancy foreign muck. We have heard of sushi in the West Midlands.

18. If your church is infested with death-watch beetle you could even kill two birds with one stone. While I can't vouch for the palatability of death-watch beetles, I have it on good authority (my younger son) that ants "taste of lemon".

Chapter 21
FOOTBALL 20

Armchair Sport of the Week

Mind Travel

In the depths of December, when the rain beats on our window panes and we still haven't bought all the Christmas presents or sprinkled glitter on the cobwebs to give the house a festive feel, this is the time to envy the lucky souls who live in the southern hemisphere. I may not be able, physically, to catch a flight back to New Zealand this week, but there's nothing to stop me travelling there in my mind's eye. Why, I can even afford to travel Club Class that way!

****[19]

So here I am again, sitting watching the sun set over Wellington Harbour. This morning I watched a large luxury cruiser come slowly in and dock here until the evening. At 6pm with a disdainful hoot of its horn it made its way sedately off, leaving me with the comforting thought that the rich, too, may suffer sea sickness.

Throughout the day the various inter-island ferries come and go. The sea is never the same for two hours at a time. Sometimes, like this morning, it is as flat as a millpond, and you can almost see the

---

19. That row of asterisks was to create the impression of time passing, rather than to shield your eyes from an expletive. Polite newspapers like to do the latter, in case some impressionable child happens to glance at the page. This way the child can sit there puzzling, "F***. Hmm. What can *that* possibly mean?"

reflections of the mountains on the opposite side of the bay, just as if this were a calm lake and not the sea at all. Every time I glance up from my work, I can see the bay and the constantly changing light and water. This morning I saw a pod of killer whales playing in the water down below. And now...

Stop this madness! There are still Christmas cards to write. Let me console myself with the thought that there were bad things about that whole New Zealand experience, too. Terrible things. Like earthquakes.

Extreme Sport

Living on a Fault Line

Wellington, New Zealand's capital city, is built on a fault line. I asked a local why it was that the city was built here, of all places, and she said that the theory was that the first settlers were blown into the harbour by the wind and couldn't get out again. But to be honest, when I sat looking out across the bay, I could understand why. It's like San Francisco. At a distance you think they must be bonkers to build here, but once you see it, you fall in love with the place and it all makes sense. The fabulous Wellington museum, Te Papa, is specially designed to be earthquake-proof. For all I know, the rest of the buildings – including the one I trustingly lived in for three months – are all built in some cunning, shock-absorbent way.

But I can't help fearing this isn't *entirely* true. I remember noticing the local custom of building wooden – that's right, folks! wooden! – decks on stilts jutting out over the abyss, to park your car on, with steps leading down to your house in the gorge below. Now, I don't know about you, but I wouldn't want my fear of earthquakes in general to be compounded by the thought that if a big one comes along, the first thing I will know about it will be the sudden arrival of my car through my tin roof from a great height. Doesn't that *worry* people at all? Or do they just not think about it? Do they live their lives on the gamble that there won't be a major quake in their lifetime? It's not that people are unaware of the risks. Earthquakes down there have the habit of reconfiguring the entire landscape, not just rattling the teacups.

But we all live with risk. Americans used to wonder how we Brits lived with the constant threat of terrorist attacks. I suppose the answer is that you live as best you can, acknowledging the danger, being sensible and trusting to whatever you trust – good luck or the Good Lord.

Biblical Sporting Hero of the Week

Jonah – who took the idea of swimming with dolphins to its logical conclusion.

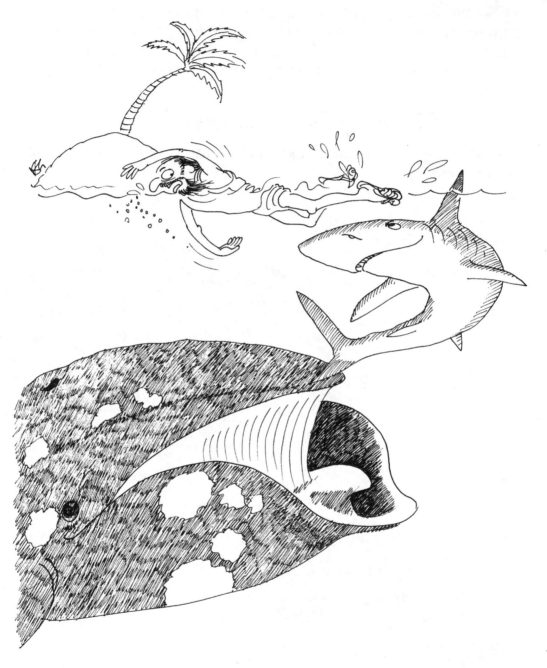

"Mostly they taste of locusts and wild honey, but mind the Old Testament ones — they're as sour as lemons."

Chapter 22
FOOTBALL 21
FA Third Round Sunday

Extreme Everyday Sport

Shopping; Sub-event: The January Sales

This major national tournament attracts some of our best retail athletes who dazzle us with their performances in a wide range of events. Some of the most popular are:

- overnight queuing
- Marks & Spencer returns queue
- driving round the car park looking for a space nearest to the store[20]
- catfighting in the handbag department[21]
- tantrums[22]
- ruining people's lives[23]

Great Sporting Challenges of our Time – Handling Personal Debt

This, along with binge-drinking and vomit-skating, is currently our nation's biggest challenge. This is partly because self-denial is old-

---

20. Men.
21. Women.
22. Under fives.
23. Parents of teenagers. See below, *Parent Power*.

fashioned. It is so-o-o last century, as the young people say. These days we should have what we want NOW, *because we're worth it.* Huge numbers of people in this country are in debt as a result of this belief. Every so often I get nice letters from my credit card company joyfully bringing me the news that they are raising my credit limit, due to my "exemplary account management". Loosely translated as, "Hmm, we don't seem to be getting much in the way of interest payments out of you, so let's see if we can entice you into some retailing folly."

People of my parents' and grandparents' generation used to regard it as a moral failing to go overdrawn. I tend to take it for granted. What I don't take for granted is having thousands of pounds worth of debt on several different cards. My basic premise is that if I can't afford it this month, I can't afford it. Even if I do deserve it or need cheering up.

Extreme Retail Therapy

We all joke about shopaholics, but I was interested to read that for some people this is a real addiction. They feel low, so they go out shopping and spend a small fortune on clothes and handbags, feel good for about three minutes, then plunge into guilt, stuff the bags into the bottom of the wardrobe and forget about them, till the Visa bill arrives and they feel low, so they go out shopping, and so on.

In my thoughtful way, I believe I've come up with a solution here. What we need is a retail therapy unit where you can go and buy a bunch of covetable things. You then make your way to the unit coffee shop and have a celebratory cappuccino and a chocolate croissant, your designer carrier bags clustered glossily at your feet. You experience 20 minutes of gloating consumer bliss. After this, just before the guilt and misery sets in, you make your way to a special desk and return all your goods and have the amount refunded onto your credit card. This service will cost you £5, and as you leave, you will be presented with a choice of either a bottle of wine, a bunch of flowers or a box of Belgian chocolates. *Et voilà* – the perfect retailing expedition for the cost of a fiver and a cup of coffee. Plus a free gift!

Martial Art of the Week

Parent Power

When children are tiny, parents generally have considerable power. If the worst comes to the worst you can pick the child up, tuck it under your arm, and take it wherever you please. As time passes, the balance of power starts its stealthy shift in the child's favour, until you end up with a hulking teenager who can no longer be carted about the place without recourse to restraining devices and heavy lifting gear. At this point, new strategies are called for.

Perhaps the most effective is The Embarrassment Factor. Most parents have in the wardrobe at least one item of clothing (usually a hat of some kind or something pink) that can be employed as crowd control. Parents who are clergy have another weapon in their arsenal: "I'm going to phone your headteacher and offer to take an assembly." When your child is small, it is a matter of some pride if Dad or Mum comes into school and juggles / eats dog food / accidentally sets fire to the main hall curtains while leading assembly. Not so at high school, where it comes in just ahead of the public face-wash with the spitty hanky.

Chapter 23
FOOTBALL 22

Great Sporting Challenges of our Time

Getting Your Money's Worth from Gym Membership

Most gyms work on the principle that they will get a huge surge of new members in the New Year, but that by the end of January, when those resolutions are wearing thin, and liposuction is beginning to look like a better option, numbers will drop back to normal levels. The way the finances work is that a handful of fitness fanatics is being underwritten by large numbers of slobs. Slobs are the seven-eighths of the gym membership iceberg. The only way to make it work for you is to find a pay-as-you-go gym.

Health and Diet

Beer, the Health-giver

One of my theories about health and fitness is that if you wait patiently enough, every vice will eventually be endorsed by new research from a team at the University of Narnia. "Good news for all smokers – cigarettes are good for you!" I think that's the only headline we are still waiting for. Even beer got the thumbs up a year or so ago, when we learned that beer drinking doesn't cause a beer gut.[24]

Yes, beer has joined red wine, coffee and chocolate in the list of items jumping from deadly sin to cardinal virtue category in one agile

---

24. Or, as this is a polite Christian paperback on sale in America, a beer *tummy*.

leap. This research carried out in the Czech Republic by a team from University College London announced that "The association between beer and obesity, if it exists, is probably weak." If this is true, then there will now be a linguistic vacuum. We will have to start referring to "an unhealthy lifestyle belly" instead.

Fitness Regimes

Moderation: The Anglican Way

Even better news was the research indicating that vigorous exercise wasn't actually any better than moderate exercise as an aid to weight loss. I think this is immensely cheering. Every time people groan to themselves, *I really must get more exercise*, they go and read some stern pronouncement which says, *Thou shalt do at least five sessions of strenuous exercise a week*! Human nature being what it is, the response is one of despair. But now we know that going for a walk is about as effective as a session at the gym.

Let's face it, the gym can be a scary place. I know lots of women are terrified by weights in particular. I overheard another mum at the school gates announcing to her friend that she'd had to stop doing weights, as she was getting too muscly. All I can say is that she'd cunningly camouflaged them under a layer of flab. I'd go for muscles every time, but that's just personal preference.

Let's address this odd fear head-on. Three biceps curls, women seem to think, and huge muscles will suddenly burst out of my arms like airbags and I'll end up looking like Popeye. Well, sorry – that's just not going to happen. You need testosterone for that, and most of us don't have enough to grow a decent moustache.

Armchair Sport

Pragmatic Etymology

All that's required for this gentle sport is a good dictionary. Remember, you are not seeking the root of the word alone. You need also to apply it to its particular social context. Take women's fear of muscles. My dictionary informs me that that the word "muscle" comes from the Latin *musculus*, meaning "little mouse", from the imagined resemblance of some muscles to mice. This would mean that the fear is a climbing-on-chairs-clutching-your-skirts kind of phobia (as in *Shriek! A mouse!*). I'm not convinced by the resemblance, I confess. Maybe I should test it out on the blokes at the judo club: "Oi, mush! Your muscles look like little mice!"

I'll report back. From my hospital bed.

Chapter 24

FOOTBALL 23

Extreme Shallowness

This is becoming something of an art form in our jaded postmodern world. Nowhere is this seen more clearly than in our endless quest for youth and beauty. Personal grooming, beauty treatments, fashion, football even! may now be canvassed as topics meriting serious thought. By the same token, subjects once considered grave and weighty may now be treated flippantly. "Shallow" is the new "deep". Broadly speaking, the main thrust of any discussion nowadays may be cogently summarised in the popular Youth Word, "Whatever".

Take, for example, a piece of serious research conducted at Oxford Brookes University into stiletto heels. Stiletto heels are a kind of icon of girlie shallowness, yet they may be approached scientifically. I'm afraid the results heralded a bad day for parents hoping to stop their daughters dressing like strumpets. They showed that wearing stiletto heels is no more likely to cause arthritic knee problems than wearing sensible shoes. Worse still, the high heel "may actually protect against" arthritis. Up and down the country 13-year-old girls will now have an answer to the old parental favourite, "You're not going out looking like *that*!" "But Mummy, I'm guarding against arthritis!"

The Enshallowment of Classical Music

"Please hold for an operator. Your call is valuable to us. So much so that we are now going to play you Vivaldi's *Four Seasons*!" These days everyone is cultured.[25] Classical music is everywhere. I was in a salon for a spot of waxing the other day – which is what we Protestants do instead of flagellation – and they were playing some Tavener. Health spas are normally more into the "Richard Clayderman plays Mozart in the rainforest" kind of background music, with lots of tinkling riffs and exotic bird calls. This is to make the experience of waxing so enjoyable that you think, "Hey, while I'm here why don't I get them to pull all my toenails out, as well?"

We must not be deluded into thinking that music is provided for the customers' enjoyment. A sinister piece of research a while back revealed that "restaurateurs wishing to increase their patrons' willingness to part with cash should play classical music to them". This is the conclusion drawn from an experiment conducted in a restaurant in Leicestershire. Takings were £2 a head less when pop music was played, and down even further when no music was played at all. Beethoven would roll over in his grave.

The Enshallowment of Religious Iconography

A while ago I bought a striking Sacred Heart wastepaper bin from Poundland. Now, I'd be the first to confess to an ignorance (bordering on bigotry) of Roman Catholic piety, but I did wonder what use the manufacturers had in mind for these bins when they rolled off the production line.

I was similarly puzzled by the Pope snowstorm a friend brought back from the Vatican. Perhaps kitschiness has some sacred function unknown to mere Protestants? I'm told there is a crucifix hologram at Willenhall Comprehensive School. As you walk past, Jesus' eyes close in death, but if you stop at a certain point, he appears to wink at you from the cross. Some time ago the religious studies block burned down, *but the picture miraculously survived*. It's a bit warped, but it apparently still winks as you walk past it. I think we may have the makings of a modern shrine on our hands: The Winking Jesus of Willenhall.

---

25. Except possibly my spellcheck, which suggested I might mean "Invalid's" *Four Seasons* – flu, hay fever, sunstroke and pneumonia?

"Hmm, it may have been a mistake to let Ozzie Osborne join the choir."

Chapter 25
FOOTBALL 29

FA Fourth Round Sunday

―――――

Mental Workout

When it comes to our mental faculties it's a question of "use it or lose it". This is certainly my observation when it comes to mathematical abilities. At some stage I must have been able to work out angles and do long division. For goodness' sake, we had to master log tables and slide rules in my day. It's just that this knowledge has fallen into a cerebral black hole, along with my National Insurance number.

The difficulties come when I'm asked to help people with their maths homework. I really don't expect to have to spend my time doing takeaways (unless they are from the local Balti house) at my stage of life. By the time he was ten, my older son was far more numerate than I am. Before long I'll be paying him to do my tax form for me. He's blessed with a phenomenal memory, and where memory is under pressure, he invents useful mnemonics. I still remember the one he made up for the order of the planets: "My very eccentric mother juggles saucepans up near Pleck."[26] I wasn't sure whether to applaud his ingenuity, or clout him round the head. With a saucepan.

Remembering things – if only I had a useful mnemonic for my lifestyle. I fear it would become hopelessly long before I'd got out of the door in the morning. Remembering to get up, washed and dressed,

―――――

26. This is an area of Walsall. Every time I go there now, I clap my hand to my forehead and say, "I've forgotten my saucepans!" My son doesn't find this amusing.

eat breakfast, provide the correct breakfast for my children, make the packed lunch and put the correct sandwiches in the correct box with the correct flavour of crisp and type of squash, remembering the PE and/or swimming kit, locating the important letter from school which has to be in today with £4 and without which the world will end... This is just the first hour of the day and already we have a vast, unwieldy mnemonic which begins, "Underwear wobble detonators become blinking fatuous, 'cos pyromaniac Latinos blast cardboard scooters practically everywhere" – which is a nice picture, but doesn't really help us get to grips with life.

Maybe we should return to basics and cling to the little mnemonic we all learned in Sunday School to the tune of "Jingle Bells": "J-O-Y, J-O-Y, surely this must mean: Jesus first, yourself last, and others in between."

Extreme Everyday Sport

Dodge-the-Dog-Poo

This is a sport that particularly appeals to parents of small children. I used to play it a lot when I walked both my sons to school through Walsall's arboretum. The basic technique is to take each child firmly by the hand and jerk them viciously around any excrement you spot on the pavement. They are then supposed to yell accusingly, "I SAW IT!!" or "Mu-u-um! You almost made me step in it!" There was a TV advert a while back for some kind of Walt Disney's *Winnie the Pooh* merchandise: "We've looked all over the Thousand Acre Wood and we can't find Pooh anywhere!" My sons used to hoot with laughter every time it was on. Piglet should try looking in Walsall Arboretum, was the feeling.

It's important to bear in mind that our enemy here is not the humble domestic dog. When Bonfire Night approaches, we should not rejoice at the thought of Fido crouched in terror as fireworks boom all around. Our target should be the irresponsible dog owner. And while we're on the subject of fireworks, I would like to see a new type developed, a kind of smart missile which would scoop up the poop, follow the culprit home, then explode all over their front porch. I'd call it "The Revenge of the Pedestrian".

Chapter 26
FOOTBALL 25

Great Sporting Challenges of our Day

Facing Your Fears

Fear has its place in sport. It gives us that adrenalin surge which enables us to perform better than we would under terror-free circumstances. Fear is a good servant but a bad master, however. There are times when we need to confront our fears and defeat them.

Several years ago my younger son manfully overcame his bee phobia. I'm not sure it counts as a true phobia, if phobias are supposed to be irrational. Bees can inflict pain, especially killer bees from South America, coming soon to a town near you, courtesy of global warming.[27] My own spider phobia is irrational. In this country, at any rate, spiders are harmless to humans. Unless you are an old woman and swallow one and, after a long and tedious progression up the food chain, end up swallowing a horse and dying. My older son kindly informs me that the venom of English house spiders is among the most deadly in the world. It's just that their teeth can't puncture human skin.[28]

One Sunday we arrived at church to see the most enormous spider skittering around the dais at the front on stilts. As I was wearing loose-legged trousers and doing the intercessions I was quite keen that it be disposed of. I could see myself giving way to blood-curdling

---

27. Actually, I made that up. But it could happen.
28. He's making that up. Well, I hope he is.

shrieks halfway through the sick list. Hmm, thinks the congregation. Doris must be more poorly than we realised.

Happily, a VIK came and *picked it up in his bare hand*, obviously not knowing about the deadly venom thing. I didn't ask what he did with it. Chucked it over the banisters onto latecomers below, probably. This is one of the advantages of having a worship space on the second floor.[29]

Extreme Baking

Olympic Fairy-cake icing

No vicar's wife is worthy of the title if she – or he! – cannot rustle up a batch of fairy cakes. (You will notice that I say "he" as well as "she". This is to be inclusive and politically correct. These days plenty of vicars are women, so let's not forget all those male "vicar's wives" soldiering on despite being frequently overlooked and marginalised. Don't worry your beardy little heads, gentlemen. We know you work jolly hard too! And it's very much appreciated! There is nothing in the Bible to say that you can't be nearly as good at baking and fancywork as your sisters, so chin up!)

Now then, fairy cakes. Get out two bun tins and line them with bun cases. Knock up a batch of sponge mixture. Any good recipe book should have one. Put a teaspoonful of this mixture into each bun case and…la la la. You know the kind of thing. Bake them. When they are cool, ice them in pretty pastel colours and decorate with interesting sprinkly things. These might include hundreds-and-thousands, sugar flowers, the tops of iced gems (bite the biscuit off first), crystallised violets, mini eggs and tiny metal ball-bearings. The latter look exactly like those little silver balls, and I find they make a nice mischievous alternative.

NB You will find that there is quite a bit of mixture left over, so make another half-dozen buns with it. If you disobeyed my instruction about only putting a teaspoon of mixture in each case, you

---

29. There is a coffee shop on the middle floor, and once upon a time at a funeral, the undertakers pressed the wrong button in the lift. The café manager soon put them right as they began to unload the coffin, so no harm done.

will discover to your cost that the cake overflows its case and spills out like the wrath of God upon a sinful world (if you come from a Nonconformist background) or like cake mixture out of a bun case (if you are an Anglican).

Chef's Tip: Fairy cake decorating is a precise science. You don't want small children mucking it up. They will see you at work and try to "help". You must – gently but firmly – scream, "Push off, push off! *I'M* doing this!" and elbow them away, otherwise they will ruin your carefully planned colour schemes, and you will be too embarrassed to take the results to the bring-and-buy.

Chapter 27
FOOTBALL 26

Extreme Shallowness

Surgical Enhancement

A few years back, there was some intense debate about whether or not Kylie had had cosmetic surgery on her bum. I never did find out whether that meant implants of some kind. I found the idea a bit baffling. Don't most of us want to be *smaller* in this department? I thought that was what liposuction was all about. Or maybe that's for thighs. I've just decided to pioneer a new form of cosmetic surgery called lipomigration, where fat is hoovered out of your thighs and transplanted in your buttocks, because, frankly, would you trust an implant to bear your weight? Imagine sitting down heavily for the intercessions and having your new backside go off with a loud report. Or worse still, what if, on April Fool's Day, some joker put a drawing pin on your pew, causing you to fly backwards round the worship area as you deflated?

Extreme Anglicanism

Ballooning: A Liturgical Approach

One Easter a VIK bought six gold and silver helium-filled balloons to decorate the church. These came from our wonderful local party shop, Swinnertons (Purveyors of Fine Stink Bombs to the Sons of the Clergy). They also sell dove-shaped balloons, so that's Pentecost sorted, too. This led me to think that there may be a gap in the market here for a Liturgical Balloon Company (For All Your Worship-related

"We're just devastated — she drowned in her own nail polish."

Helium Needs!). Balloons in the shape of paschal candles, an entire helium-filled crib set, inflatable bishops for confirmations and ordinations…the lists goes on and on. After the service any leftover helium should, of course, be disposed of irreverently, eg inhaled prior to a rendition of "Jesus wants me for a sunbeam" or another Sunday School classic of your choice.

Liturgical Slimming

Many of us will have noticed adverts in the colour supplements for home exercise equipment. You know the kind: "Get Trim and Wear Bikini in Minutes" exercise systems. I know some people have a loft full of them.

A curate I know once bought an exercise bike. The accompanying literature suggested he measure his waist before embarking on the regime, which he did – with a steel tape. (This is apparently fine if you warm it up on the radiator first.) He read up on different fitness schemes. One offered "The Six-week Beach Body". However, what he felt he needed was "The Two-week Baptism Body", as he was facing the prospect of an adult baptism by full immersion job at the local baths.

Extreme Vanity

A Christian Approach to the Eyebrow

There is no need to spend lots of money on eyebrow grooming. Very good results can be achieved at home, and the money you save could be donated to some deserving cause. You may know some struggling writer, for instance, who would be glad of the cash.

Gents: Ideally, what we are looking for is not The Eyebrow at all, but two separate eyebrow entities. The mono-brow is not unusual, but can present a bad-tempered appearance. To achieve two eyebrows, simply pluck or shave the half-inch patch above the bridge of your nose, or get your gardener to do this for you.

Another feature of eyebrows is that they become more luxuriant with each passing year, rather like a mature shrub. Your barber (or gardener) can easily mow them for you with his buzzer/strimmer next time you go for a cut. You may, on the other hand, wish to cultivate rampant growth.[30]

Ladies: I don't recommend the same gardening equipment in your daily toilette. Here's my hint for eyebrows that are getting out of control: comb them downwards (a nit comb is ideal for this) and trim them carefully with your very *special* own *private* pair of *really sharp* needlework scissors that HAVE NOT BEEN USED TO CUT THOSE PLASTIC TAGS THAT HOLD HUB CAPS ON.[31]

---

30. Indeed, gargantuan eyebrows are sometimes considered requisite for high office in the Church of England.
31. Really sharp needlework scissors which have been blunted in this way need not be thrown out. They can always be used to cut up the sports pages of the newspaper before other people have had a chance to read them.

THE SEASON OF RUGBY

(Colour: blood)

How my spirits rise when the Season of Rugby approaches! If we are being strictly honest, the season of football doesn't end here, it is merely interrupted – and gloriously! – by a higher sporting form. No modern theologian is in any doubt that you are closer to God on a rugby pitch than anywhere else on earth.[32] Rugby embodies many of the great Christian virtues, such as not whining. Contrast it with football. One little tap on the ankle and your prima donna striker is writhing on the pitch in hope of being awarded a penalty. Rugby players have to be positively *ordered* off the pitch if they are injured. Even then, they just go to the touchline to have their trailing limb stitched back on, chafing the whole time at not being in the thick of the action.

A rugby match is essentially an 80-minute prophetic act against the compensation culture. It is our duty as Christians to support it.

---

32. Except possibly when you are running back and forth across a busy motorway.

"*Darling, it's not the getting injured that counts,
it's the taking part.*"

Chapter 28
SIX NATIONS SUNDAY
(FOOTBALL 27)
or FA Fifth Round Sunday

═══════════════

Rugby: A Theological Analysis

Great theologians of both East and West are united in their view that rugby is a more spiritual sport than football. It is the opinion that I myself hold. The thesis draws on observations of the elevated principles rugby embodies and the manly and character-building ethos of the game. And those incredibly sexy tight shirts they wear these days. Some people think. Apparently. I can't say I'd particularly noticed their contour-hugging properties.

Another trait of rugby, which is very much to the sport's credit, is its ability to draw fresh minds into the ongoing spiritual debate. For example, a midwife I know suggests the game would be improved if both teams wore nothing but body paint and g-strings. This is an interesting and important proposal, awaiting expression in German before it is taken seriously in the academic community.[33] My personal view is that it would make hoisting a player by his shorts in the line-out impracticable.

As the 2003 Rugby World Cup progressed, religious philosophers up and down the country were quick to notice that the new-style

───────────────

33. *Flickschuster* (Cobblers) might well be the word. It would apply equally well to the prosperity gospel.

shirts could be ripped off. This revealed, a little to my surprise, that the entire pack now seem to wear sports bras. I expect there's a reason for this. Gone a little too far with that muscle definition, probably.

Mental Workout

Everything comes to those who wait. If we are diligent in scouring our daily papers we will eventually be rewarded with news of some groundbreaking research that justifies our favourite vice. This was true when *The Times* brought a gleam to the eye of the pub-goer. "Spending more time at the pub could actually be good for your brain." Unless it is a very quaint olde worlde hostelry with low beams. These can be bad for the brain if you are over five-foot-ten tall.

So "Bottoms up", say the team of researchers from University College London. They discovered "a direct link between going to the pub and improved verbal and numerical ability". I imagine this comes partly from the stimulation of having to remember a round of drinks for the space of time between asking people what they want, and getting served at the bar. This is a skill which eludes me. I can't always remember whether I want tea or coffee as I stand in my own kitchen.

The numerical side would be to do with totting up the cost and checking the change, another ability I don't have, but which I gloss over by slipping 20 quid to a VIK and letting him buy the drinks. It's a choice between looking useless by colluding with patriarchy, or looking useless by floundering at mental arithmetic. Bimboism requires less effort, so it's basically a wise deployment of mental energy, freeing up resources which can then be channelled into other activities.[34] I don't feel bad about being innumerate, by the way. As my older son points out, there are three types of people in this world: those who can count, and those who can't.

Obviously the researchers must have been looking only at people who drink in moderation. Getting off your face notoriously impairs your verbal skills. This is why I never drink and write. If I did, the page I'm working on would look something like this: 5k,m;9 7ri .®;78p5t t7r[[[[[[[[[[[[[[[[[[[– which is what happens if you slump forwards and your face lands on the keyboard. (I rolled around a bit to

---

34. Like wondering if you're too old for leather trousers.

simulate what I imagine drunken stupor to be like.) To be fair, though, the team wished to emphasise that it was the social, not the alcoholic, aspect of pub visits which imparted the benefit. No doubt you could get similar results from tea shops or breaking up into small groups on church study days.

Chapter 29
RUGBY 2 (FOOTBALL 28)

Extreme Parenting

Chauffeuring the Children

Our older son went to Germany on a school trip earlier in the year. The coach left at one in the morning, and a VIK kindly volunteered to be the 24-hour taxi service. This is a fair division of labour. After all, I was the one who got up to feed them in the small hours when they were tiny. It seems entirely appropriate that someone else should do the late-night ferrying around so that I can catch up on my lost sleep. Except I didn't, of course. I kept getting up and asking if he'd remembered his pyjamas and whether he'd like a travel sickness tablet. The maternal martyr role is a hard one to shed.

I suppose the parental taxi service is something we'll have to get used to. Given that most parents lie awake waiting for the sound of their child returning, we might as well be taxiing them home. The idea is that if we're nice and drive our son around now, he will drive us around when he's passed his test, so that we can skip the "Shall I drive, darling? Oh silly me, I've just absentmindedly knocked back a treble gin!" routine every time we go out somewhere.

Mental Workout

Opera

It scarcely seems a moment since my own first trip to Germany in 1977. I was on an exchange visit to Stuttgart. Among the many exciting and educational excursions organised by my host family was a trip to the famous Stuttgart ballet. My penfriend and I sat in the dress circle in a state of high excitement as the curtain went up. Two dancers were already poised on the stage. If the woman seemed a little stouter than is usual for a prima ballerina, it didn't strike me as particularly odd. This was Germany, after all. However, when she opened her lips and sang, my astonishment was complete. I can still picture my penfriend's open-mouthed disbelief. Just to spare you a similar surprise, Tchaikovski's *Eugene Onegin* is actually an *opera*. And to clear up another popular misconception, it has barely started when the fat lady sings. I'm afraid that some 28 years later I have still not truly learned to love opera. The same is true for brain soup, I'd have to say.

Armchair Sport of the Week

Hearts

If you are a truly sad person, you will know at once who Pauline, Ben and Michele are. In fact, you probably spend an unhealthy amount of time in their company. For those of you not addicted to computer card games, this trio is who you pit your wits against in Microsoft Hearts. A while back, just for a bit of variety, a VIK changed the names. For several months he could be found locked in debate with Luther, Calvin and Zwingli. More recently – perhaps because it was spring at the time and the pheromones are raging, who knows? – I discovered he's been closeted in his study with Jordan, Kylie and Beyoncé. Sometimes I fear for the Church of England. I really do.

"*Calm down, officers, it's only virtual poker.*
I've virtually won and they've virtually no money left."

Chapter 30
RUGBY 3 (FOOTBALL 29)

Extreme Sport

Survival Guides

The more extreme white-knuckle junkies among us will be forever seeking out new thrills and exposing themselves to dangers that we timid folk may never encounter. This doesn't mean that we don't like to be informed about such matters. Last Christmas we were given a "Worst-case Scenario" calendar with a page to a day given over to matters of survival. The "how to survive" tips range from "alien abduction" (go for their eyes) to "how to clamber along the top of a moving train" (if you see a bridge coming, duck). As the months have gone by I've become convinced that there is room for a clergy worst-case scenario guide.

How to survive if your surplice catches fire during communion

Firstly, don't panic. If the wine is not yet consecrated, tip it on the blaze. If you have already said the prayer of consecration, signal discreetly to the verger, who will beat the flames out with a hassock. If the verger is deep in prayer, has nipped outside for a fag, or is otherwise unavailable, announce a hymn[35] and roll in a dignified manner across the chancel floor until the flames are smothered. Once the blaze is under control, continue the service. The most important thing is to carry on as though nothing has happened. In the unlikely

---

35. eg "Come down, O love divine", "O thou who camest from above", "Shine, Jesus, shine", all of which contain suitable imagery.

event of fire ripping through the robed choir, evacuate the building and lead a calm procession to the village pond.

How to survive at the crem when you have packed a double-bed sheet instead of a surplice

Fold the sheet into quarters. Borrow a Swiss Army knife and cut the middle out of the sheet to make a hole slightly larger than your head. Drape this over your cassock, poncho-style. If possible, borrow a stapler or some sticky tape and fasten the side seams together, but if neither is available, don't worry, just try not to wave your arms around too much.

How to survive an unexpected episcopal visit to the vicarage

If you have reason to believe you are in your bishop's bad books, or he is a frothing psychopath, on no account open the door. Sit tight until he goes away. If he knows you are in, or you hear the sound of him jemmying the door with his crosier, pick up your credit card and leave swiftly and silently at the rear of the house and escape through the neighbouring gardens/fields. Leave the country until the fuss has died down.

What to do if an important football match coincides with Evensong

The key word here is "delegation", or, to employ current good church practice jargon, "enabling" (as in "enabling the process of every-member ministry"). To assume that every service requires the presence of an ordained minister is an outmoded "pale male" (ie white, patriarchal) model of "doing church". Sexism and rigid hierarchy are no longer acceptable, even in Evangelicalism, so make sure you have at least one "super Christian girl" (ie pretty) or "dear sister" (not pretty) training as a lay reader. That way she can take over on match nights, when the congregation will probably be small so it won't matter.

Chapter 31

RUGBY 4 (FOOTBALL 30)

Sport of the Week

Extreme Contraception

I'm beginning to think that the sport of extreme contraception needs to be recognised officially. The so-called "Vatican Roulette" method of natural family-planning has existed for years and is already regarded in some circles as an extreme sport. As doctors are fond of pointing out, there is a well-known medical term for people using the rhythm method. They are called "parents".

Another contender for the title must be sterilisation. In theory this event is open to both genders, but for medical reasons it is not generally advised for men, despite its being a minor procedure carried out under local anaesthetic. This is because a vasectomy is like tying a knot in the barrel of a shotgun. In due course the man's testicles will explode. Everyone knows *that*.

Which leads me to my main reason for suggesting a new sporting category – the salutary case of David Walker reported in our papers a while back, who shot himself in the testicles after sticking a sawn-off shotgun in his pocket. He was apparently intending to "sort his friend out" after a drunken argument. Besides losing both testicles, Walker faces up to five years in prison for possessing an illegally modified weapon.

So be very careful what you carry around in your pockets, boys![36]

---

36. Even if it's only a mobile phone. There is research into the fertility of men who regularly carry and use mobile phones which suggests that their sperm count can be cut by up to 30%. The theory is that it's the radiation emitted by mobile phones which causes the damage.

Extreme Happiness

This is, of course, a bloodsport. People will pursue happiness quite ruthlessly. Indeed, if you are American, it is your constitutional right to do so – and sue the pants off anyone who impedes you in the chase. Like many sports it can be expensive, though, as a piece of research undertaken by economists at Warwick University amply demonstrated: "We calculate that to turn a normal Briton into a very happy one by means of money alone, it would take a minimum of £1m."

I didn't know about this when my older son was in his last weeks of junior school and feeling the big black cloud of high school looming on the horizon – fortunately, as I didn't have a spare million to hand at that moment. Instead, I gave him a little pep-talk about happiness and tried gently to help him see things in perspective. "Get a grip. A hundred and fifty years ago children your age were working down the mines!" Not really. What I actually said was that lots of grown-ups spend all their time thinking that they will be happy when x or y has happened. The sad thing is that happiness is always something in the future, never the present.

At the time, I used to watch him and his younger brother playing their elaborate imaginary games on the way to school, and was reassured that they still had the capacity to live in the present moment and enjoy it to the full.[37] It's very natural, when things are going badly, to say with the Psalmist, "Oh, that I had the wings of a dove! I would fly away and be at rest!" The trouble is that faith just ain't like that. Our sport isn't escapism, it's endurance. The clue here is the cross.

---

37. Not that I began to understand their games. For example, here is a snippet I overheard once: "Uh-oh! I don't like the look of this – get your coconuts out!" (*Only* try this at home, ladies.)

Chapter 32
FOOTBALL 31

Survival Event of the Week

Staying in a Welsh Cottage

Part i) Gaining access

Every now and then we spend a happy week in a cottage a few miles outside Llangollen. Last time, before we set off, I asked the owners what we ought to take with us, and they said bed linen, towels and a crowbar for jemmying the front door. We don't own a crowbar here in the vicarage so I had to borrow one from a midwife I know. She has three, which I believe she uses in her private rather than her professional capacity, but admittedly, it's a long time since I last saw the inside of a labour ward. Traditional methods of delivery were very much in vogue a decade ago, birthing stools and so on, so perhaps some form of medieval crowbar obstetrics has made a comeback. But, as the young people say, let's not go there.

It turned out that we didn't need the crowbar after all. The keys did the trick. But it was a wise precaution as the door opens outwards, rendering useless the more conventional shoulder barge method of opening swollen doors.

Part ii) Surviving without a TV

The week was a sort of social experiment in what happens to children aged ten and twelve when they are severed from technology for whole hours at a time. As predicted, they were forced to fall back on primitive methods of amusing themselves, such as reading, drawing, exploring the local streams and hills and whining, "Mu-u-um! He's *annoying* me!" We made the occasional daring foray into Llangollen when rustication got the better of us. This made it possible to *spend money*, the only activity which validates a trip in the eyes of ten- and twelve-year-olds.

In previous years, holidays in Llangollen were popular because of the steam trains, but we are now wa-a-ay too old for Thomas the Tank Engine. These days the Fat Controller means me telling them they can't have another packet of crisps. But it takes a few years to catch up. I've only just stopped pointing out diggers and waving at firemen. Fortunately Llangollen holds other attractions, the main one being the taxidermist's shop. "Cool! Dead things!" According to my older son, there are three things boys of his age are interested in: mobile phones, computer games and dead things.

You know, I sometimes think that there is something in the theory that women are from Venus and boys are from The Planet of Rotting Zombie Flesh. Growing up as one of four girls, I can tell you that we had a totally different take on the subject. We mourned for days if we saw a car run over an already dead baby bird. We would have shed bitter tears if we'd seen the bloated corpse of a rabbit floating in the canal at the Froncysyllte aqueduct. Our concern would be whether we could fish it out and give it a decent burial, not waiting eagerly to see if it would be shredded by the propeller of a passing narrow boat.

Extreme Anglicanism

Sermon Feedback

The writer Don Marquis once said that "publishing a volume of verse is like dropping a rose petal down the Grand Canyon and waiting for an echo". There are many preachers who would be tempted to apply this to their experience of delivering a sermon. Some churchgoers feel that it is enough to refrain from audible snoring. This is a good starting point, of course, but a bit of genuine feedback is even better.

"And finally, the churchwardens are offering this rather nice claret to anyone who can remember three points from the sermon today... Now, let's sing the Tedium."

Chapter 33
RUGBY 5 (FOOTBALL 32)

Everyday Sport

"**E**veryday sport – everybody feels better for it." That's the new catchphrase that will shortly impinge on our consciousness from all angles. The government has realised that exhorting people to go to the gym is counter-productive in our increasingly obese society. When you are overweight a strange sense of powerlessness takes over. This is what leads us to sigh in a fatalistic way and say, "Well, I've eaten one chocolate button, I may as well eat *all* the children's Easter eggs, now." The amount of self-discipline required to make a real go of the gym is just too daunting. As often as not, our resolve is exhausted by the mere act of enrolling and buying a new pair of fancy trainers.

These are some of the government's suggestions for "everyday sport": pushing the baby's pram, gardening, getting off the bus one stop early and walking, climbing the stairs instead of using the lift. Not forgetting WALKING YOUR CHILD TO SCHOOL. That was my own addition. I'm surprised it wasn't on the list, to be honest, as it encourages children to be active as well. There is a real risk otherwise, that they will see "everyday sport" as yet another weird, sad thing adults do, like washing their hands, saying uniVERSITY, and managing to utter a statement without turning it into a question.

Low Sunday – Annual Mad Intonation Award Day

One of the sad things about being an ordained minister is the Low Sunday phenomenon. This ensures that they never sample Anglican worship at its best from the pew. They are forever destined to go on holiday after Easter/Christmas and to attend churches half empty of parishioners and sit through an act of worship led by some noble soul wheeled out of retirement for the occasion.

By way of compensation, there are the national Mad Intonation Award finals, which are generally held on Low Sunday. Up and down the land competitors may be heard in pulpit and chancel experimenting with bold new emphases in the liturgy, placing stresses where no stress has ever been placed before. "The Lord *be* with you." "Let *us offer* one *an*other a sign *of* peace." Splendid old sermons will be dusted off for the occasion; anecdotes about missionary *days* in Zaire or *of* boyhood cricket *matches* will be offered for our contemplation.

Another feature of Low Sunday is the question clergy on holiday have to pose themselves. Shall I bother going to church at all? (With its attendant sub-question: Shall I force the children to come with me?) This is a useful process to go through. It throws things into sharp relief. Is church "work", and therefore something we are exempt from on holiday? Or is it a solemn duty imposed on all believers, whether on holiday or not? Or is it pleasure? What is church *for*, exactly – for us to satisfy our personal spiritual needs? to build up the body of believers in general? or for God, to give him the honour he deserves?

Chapter 34
RUGBY 6 (FOOTBALL 33)

Away Fixtures

Now and then we venture out to worship with other denominations. For instance, my sons and I went recently with my parents to their local Baptist chapel. About a third of the way through the service the notices were announced. My older son sat up eagerly from his slumped position and whispered, "Is that it?" In our church the notices is the signal that only one more hymn has to be endured before he can go off and play football in the east room. This was not the only difference he noticed. He was baffled by the announcement, which I took utterly for granted as a fixed part of Baptist liturgy, that "the brethren will now wait upon you for your freewill offerings". Some of the confusion was cleared up when I realised he'd thought the words were, "The brethren will now wait upon you for your *feeble* offerings."

Shirt-swapping

This is a traditional part of the away fixture. At the end of the game players swap shirts so that they have a souvenir of the match. A VIK thinks that there is some scope here for shirt-swapping at the end of ecumenical services – away matches, as we think of them. Or, if the sermon has gone well, the preacher might (unless the shirt is just too tight) pull it up over his or her head and celebrate. That's "celebrate" in a sporting, not an Anglican sense, as obviously you'd need to be able to see what you were doing during the eucharistic prayer.

Extreme Anglicanism

Cathedral Processions – Getting Kitted Out

"Swimsuits and stilettos," said *The Sunday Times* "Style" magazine on the day of the ordination service. "You won't need much more this summer." Unfortunately I read this a little too late to act upon it before setting off to Lichfield Cathedral. As it turned out, nobody else seemed to be following this piece of fashion advice.

In many ways this is just as well. Lichfield Cathedral, like many other ancient churches, is not really stiletto-friendly. I'm talking about the metal grilles placed strategically in the aisles, with little holes exactly the right diameter to get your heel stuck in. This is, in fact, the only remaining argument against women bishops. It would hold up the procession if she got her Jimmy Choo jammed. Obviously it is also an argument in favour of flat soles for male bishops, but flat needn't equal frumpy. There are plenty of sweet, flirty, low-heeled styles around at the moment. Check out the polka dot ballet pumps, or the many very reasonably priced jewelled flip-flops.

Sport of the Week

Flying

In Anglican circles, this sport is only open to bishops. This is because the training is so rigorous. Ordinary lay people simply can't endure the kind of altitudes that these guys operate at.[38] So far they only compete in events where the fan base holds a certain set of beliefs (opposition to women's ordination). This is seen by many as narrow-minded, so there are moves afoot to make episcopal flying more inclusive.[39]

When the mysterious archbishop selection process was taking place a few years ago, my older son invented what must be the

---

38. Like the love of Jesus: so high, you can't get over them.
39. eg so that they can represent people opposed to gay priests. Similarly, alternative episcopal oversight ought to be made available for Newcastle fans, if their area bishop supports Sunderland.

ultimate flying bishop: Batbishop – the Coped Crusader. He hangs out in Gotham Diocese and has a chaplain called Batchap, who says things like "Holy Communion, Batbishop!"

"*I don't care what's wrong with the Batmobile. It's Holy Last Orders or you'll get nothing for tea.*"

THE SEASON OF JOYFUL HOPE

(Colour: bright)

At long last the dreadful Season of Football begins to loosen its grip. Cricket approaches with all those leisurely connotations of pastoral English life, the tock! of ball on willow, the scattered clapping, the break for tea. This is sport as it should be, sport as it will be played in heaven, following the contours of a life well-lived and stretching to fill eternity.

Chapter 35

SEXAGESIMA OR THE SECOND SUNDAY BEFORE CRICKET (FOOTBALL 34)

or British Korfball Sunday
or Semi-final Sunday

Birdspotting

The wonderful thing about birdspotting is that you can do it almost anywhere. Anywhere outdoors, of course, otherwise you are pretty much limited to budgies and the occasional surprised-looking pigeon coming in through the automatic doors at WHSmith. Before I moved to Walsall I gave way to an unworthy thought which went something like this: *Oh no! I'm going to spend the rest of my life trapped in the middle of some grim sprawling conurbation all because I married a Call to the Inner City.* This was before I discovered Walsall's wonderful arboretum.

One week when we were walking to school, my sons and I saw two lesser-spotted woodpeckers in the arboretum. The previous week it was greater-spotted, and in the distance we could hear green woodpeckers. A sort of Piciformes royal flush.[40] On my way home I

---

40. There – a day in which we learn a new word is a day not entirely wasted. Indeed, if I had bothered to look it up, I would also have learned what korfball was.

saw a pair of kingfishers. I've seen them many times, but on each new occasion I'm astonished all over again by that flash of colour. There were some Canada geese on the bank, waddling about crunching up the poppadoms someone had scattered. Waterfowl have a varied diet in a multicultural place like Walsall. On the larger lake, in defiance of the old song, there were six swans a-swimming.

When I bother to remember, I am thankful to those good Victorian people who had the vision for the arboretum, who put their hands in their pockets and made it happen, who dug and planted, knowing all along that they would never live to see its full glory.

Young Person's Sport of the Week

Collecting Yu-Gi-Oh Cards

Yu-Gi-Oh is basically Pokemon hideously transmogrified and back to haunt us just when we thought it was safe to go into town with our credit cards. I was going to create some amusing spoof names, but now I come to think about it, the originals are past satire: "Kaiser Sea Horse", "Catapult Turtle", "Mystic Tomato".

The idea is that you buy packs of these cards (or ideally your mum does), all of which turn out to be useless or swaps, and not the amazing "shiny" you have set your heart on. You then put the special ones in plastic wallets and leave them in a slithering pile in the middle of the sitting room floor in a *special order which took you hours* and which your mum will ruin when she heartlessly moves them prior to an uncharacteristic burst of vacuuming. The others you take to school in order to trade them, or to have them forcibly taken off you by a bigger meaner child and never be able to complain, because both your parents and the staff will say, "Well, you shouldn't have taken them into school, should you?"

And that is Yu-Gi-Oh, my friends. Wait, it's also a game, come to think of it. Yes, that's it – a game. That would be the point, wouldn't it? Rather than it just being a way of winkling money out of impressionable twelve-year-old boys, for example. Only a cynic would think that.

Chapter 36

QUINQUAGESIMA (FOOTBALL 35)

or the Sunday next before Cricket

Sport of the Week

Recycling

f cycling is a sport, then I can see no reason why recycling shouldn't be, perhaps with the Re-tour de France being the main event of the year.[41] Recycling is gradually catching on. Most of us at least manage the odd trip to the bottle bank, driving there in our cars, thereby (fret, fret) undoing our good environmental work. Unless we combinc it with a trip to the supermarket, of course. Where we buy lots more over-packaged stuff that ought to be recycled... It's a complex area of modern living, but at least the seed has been planted in our consciousness.

The other plus is that the bottle bank is the only place where nicely brought-up middle-class people can smash glass with impunity. A VIK and I used to smash wine glasses on a regular basis until we got a dishwasher. There is some kind of evil formula governing kitchen breakages, I've noticed. The likelihood of a glass smashing is inversely proportional to its ugliness. You can try for years – oops! clumsy me! – to break a moulded glass relish tray, and it will miraculously bounce whole off quarry tiles time after time. But the slightest chink of fragile

---

41. Won with tedious frequency by Relance Armstrong.

champagne flute against kitchen tap and the thing will shatter. Maybe there's another formula, involving the ratio of alcohol consumed to glasses smashed.

Extreme Parenting

Hosting a Sleepover[42]

This is something everyone else's parents lets them do, and therefore something you will almost certainly end up doing yourselves. I once gave permission for a double sleepover for seven thirteen-year-olds. Looking back, I could never reconstruct the exact moment when I actually agreed to this. I expect I was reading at the time. Under those circumstances I would probably give my blessing to leg amputation or voting Tory. I think I should be allowed a cooling-off period, like you are legally entitled to when you are pressurised into buying a time-share holiday.

One of the many blessings in my life is a big vicarage. Well, sometimes it's not really a blessing. When you get round to dusting, for instance. But it truly *is* a boon when you are hosting a group of snorting young people over night. For the famous double sleepover, we simply shoved them all in the sitting room and shut the door. I have no idea what time they eventually went to sleep. There's no point asking, as no child can honourably admit to something as cissy as sleeping when they could be playing cards, eating cheesy wotsits and engaging in trumpathons. On the second night it was quieter. I went for a run the following morning and peered at them through the window on my way back. They were lolling in their sleeping bags like a convention of giant comatose caterpillars.

Here is a list of things you will need if you are hosting a similar event:

- pizzas
- crisps
- fizzy drinks
- floor space
- videos
- earplugs
- large mallet
- tear gas
- air freshener
- a holiday

---

42. Or "Wakeover" as they are more accurately known.

THE SEASON OF CRICKET

(Colour: white with grass stains, with optional red stripe on trouser groin from ball polishing)

I have never played cricket myself, but someone once described it to me as long stretches of boredom punctuated by moments of sheer terror. And on a bad day, that's a pretty good description of the human lot.

Chapter 37
CRICKET 1 (FOOTBALL 36)

Nutter Sunday
being the Day of the London Marathon

Extreme Everyday Sport

Queuing

Queuing is something we must all do, alas. A recent study has shown that the British spend an average of one day a year waiting in queues – unless they are travelling to the continent when the French ferry operators are on strike, in which case it doubles. *Or* when the French farmers are mounting road blocks. It's all aimed at us, you know. *They* don't queue.

The survey also showed that the Welsh are the most likely to queue-jump. This is the fault of the chapel, I reckon. It spoils them. They've never had to queue for communion. It's always been brought round by the deacons. Personally, I never push in, despite my Welsh ancestry; though I do admit to a distinctly Cymric sprint when I'm waiting at the back of one queue at the supermarket and a new till opens nearby. I tell myself that this is a prophetic gospel act – the last shall be first, suckers!

Gender-specific Queuing Sports

Part i) Avoiding traffic queues (a male event)

A VIK has "The Knowledge" of Walsall – you know, that kind of encyclopaedic recall of all the streets that is associated with increases of hippocampus size in the brains of London cabbies. The reason he has acquired this geographical information is not primarily because of the amount of faithful pastoral visiting he has done over the last six years, so much as the result of a congenital impatience. "I don't do queues," he once told me in a grand Mariah Carey way, as we took a labyrinthinely complex route through the town centre to avoid waiting for two minutes at the big roundabout.

Part ii) Avoiding loo queues (a female event)

There is never a queue at the gents for one obvious biological reason: women have smaller bladders. That's the downside of the otherwise sensible system of wearing your reproductive apparatus on the inside. But human biology has not altered for thousands of years. Why are there *still* insufficient numbers of loos for us? A good friend of mine is so incensed by this injustice that she boldly strides into the men's loos at theatres and concert halls. I can never quite get my nerve up to follow her. Perhaps this stems from gender insecurity? As a young teenager sporting a short haircut, I was occasionally bounced from ladies' loos with the words, "Oi sonny, where do you think you're going?" I'm pleased to say this hasn't happened for several years, but the memory still keeps me queuing docilely with the girlies.

Extreme Anglicanism

Sword Drill

This is an old sport which I would like to see revived as it was something I benefited from in my youth. Like many Nonconformists, I was brought up on a diet of good old Sunday School choruses. I can still hear the cheery sound of Nellie tinkling out "In my heart there rings a melody!" on the piano, which was the signal for our small

"Barbie's going to be an architect, and she's going to design all the men's toilets at the other end of town."

classes to reconvene in the main body of the schoolroom for a spot of sword drill. I'm afraid this wasn't quite as exciting as you might think, being a rather boring matter of racing one another to look up Bible verses, rather than running Barry Bachelor through with a rapier. Those were innocent days. I seem to remember we had to stand to attention with our Bibles clamped under our left armpit, then, at the given command, brandish them menacingly aloft before riffling desperately through to find John 3:16. It may not have been a martial art as such, but it does mean I can normally find my way round the Bible without having to look at the contents page.[43]

---

43. By contrast, a VIK, who was brought up an Anglican, used to use his Bible as a table tennis bat.

Chapter 38
CRICKET 2 (FOOTBALL 37)

Feast of San Marino, patron of Grand Prix drivers, Sunday 23 April

Sport of the Week – Motor Racing

I read recently that there's a new breed of woman emerging: the girl racer. She would sooner spend her money on a fast car than a mortgage. I think this is rather dashing. I don't have temptations in that direction myself. There's no point owning a high performance car if you are only going to use it to potter into town and collide with stationary objects.

On the whole, an obsession with sporty cars remains a boy thing. It was certainly at the request of our older boy that we visited the Ferrari museum in Maranello last summer. There was an air of pilgrims visiting a holy site. Groups of men were solemnly examining shiny engines on plinths, or poring over glass cases containing a tangle of bright metal tubes that looked as though they might be the intestines of an android. Other men were taking careful photographs of cylinders, or kneeling in homage to get a good shot of the Testarossa.

I think that men don't realise that these things are not really babe magnets. If a woman looks at it longingly, the chances are she's trying to calculate what she could do with the money if she sold it.

Testosterone and the Seven Ages of Man

I concluded from our visit to the Ferrari factory that our older son was entering a new phase of male development. As far as I can see it goes something like this:

1. Diggers and tractors
2. Dinosaurs
3. Egyptians
4. Pokemon
5. Computer games
6. Fast cars
7. (from the age of thirteen till death) Sex.

A mother can no longer offer much guidance to her son as he enters the choppy waters of adolescence. She will never be completely redundant while she owns a washing machine, but at this age a boy needs male role models quite urgently. I am very grateful a VIK was on hand to explain Stage 6 and answer such questions as "What are spoilers for?" "To put on the back of perfectly good cars and spoil them". And to clarify that when we refer to a car being an extension of a man's penis, we are speaking metaphorically.

Sporting Injuries

This is something you have to take seriously if you are a true sportsperson. After a couple of years of judo I have learned to refer to my poorly toe as a "foot injury". Before each session I break out my zinc oxide tape and strap my little toes up to prevent further "injury". I occasionally wear an ankle support as well. This is nothing to what the blokes get up to. They strap on so much body armour in the way of knee supports and shoulder strapping that they resemble medieval knights preparing to joust.

But it's not just on the sports field that we encounter hazards. They assail us from all sides in everyday life. This is my central thesis in this book: life is an extreme sport. Injuries come, seemingly, from nowhere. This is what lies behind my recommendation that you always *open French windows before attempting to pass through them*. My older son enquired, after one unhappy encounter, why I hadn't checked, and I replied that there had been no need as I *knew* it was open. He pointed out gently that I couldn't have *known* this, as you can only know things which are actually true. I considered blocking his bedroom door with Plexiglas to help him grapple further with this epistemological conundrum.

Chapter 39
CRICKET 3 (FOOTBALL 38)

Armchair Sport of the Week

Reminiscence

This comes in the category of mental workouts, and is one of those sports which becomes more appealing the older you get. Just as gardening eventually becomes more compelling than sex (they tell me), so looking back becomes more interesting than looking forward. It is perfectly possible to reminisce by yourself, but this is definitely an activity that you will enjoy more if you do it with an old school friend.

For example, I wasted about half an hour once with an old mate, trying to piece together a picture of a May Ball we'd both been to at Cambridge in 1983. We discovered that we could reconstruct with confidence the venue, the outfit, the shoes, the hairstyle, *but not the partner*. We decided it revealed something about us, that we are both very shallow, trivial and vapid people, perhaps. Or that our partners were, and that's why we'd quite rightly forgotten them.

I think old friends are something like recording angels. In our fragmented postmodern age where we are free to reinvent ourselves at will, and where *our* truth is the only truth that counts, old friends pose a philosophical challenge. They can say things like, "No you haven't got O-level physics, you fat liar! You were thrown out of Mr Walsh's class for attaching him to an electric circuit with crocodile clips that week Trudy got sent off the hockey pitch for doing Spotty Dog impressions!" You can try saying, "Well, that's just *your* truth", but you know, and *they* know, that you are a liar. Much better to say, "So? *I* can remember when *you* hitchhiked all the way to Nottingham and your mother thought you were at a Shakespeare lecture in Oxford and she *still* doesn't know anything about it!"

But there's a positive side, too. You don't have to explain yourself to old friends. They can remember those childhood worries and teenage traumas which make you what you are today. They used to come for tea in the weird home you grew up in and which no longer really exists. True, you can take new friends to the geographical spot and point to the house, but you can't show them what it was like to live there in 1977. Old friends know this. Hang onto them at all costs. When you are knocked about and battered by life, "wearied by the changes and chances of this fleeting world", they bear witness to your continued ability to survive. They know you are the same you they sat next to in double maths last thing on a Friday and they will cut you some slack.

Most Hated Adult Activity

Trawling Round Charity Shops

Children hate charity shops almost as much as they hate museums. This is because they are BORING. They can therefore be used either as a form of punishment, or as a form of crowd control.

The compassionate thing is to go without them. On our day off, a VIK and I like nothing better than pottering around charity shops. Well, apart from pottering around the streets of Paris and stopping for a leisurely coffee at some boulevard café under a glorious plane tree, and watching all the beautiful *soigné* people stroll past. *Eheu!* Instead we go to nearby towns and do the charity shops. I've worked out why I like this so much. In this globalised age there are fewer and fewer interesting little shops. It's all chain stores. McDonald's, Gap, Monsoon, Starbucks – you could be anywhere. But charity shops still have a quirky charm. You never know what you're going to find there.

Chapter 40
CRICKET 4 (FOOTBALL 39)

Extreme Sport

Reading

Some of you will be surprised that I am listing reading as an extreme sport. The hazards involved aren't immediately apparent, I admit. This is because it isn't the activity itself that's risky, but the knock-on effects. Nowhere is this more true than in the realm of children's fiction, particularly with the popularity of the Harry Potter books.

I daresay it's true that a whole generation of children is growing up bent on becoming witches and wizards,[44] in much the same way that, in my day, little girls grew up determined to be ponies. We only have to look around us today to see the legacy of all those pony books that were uncritically devoured by youngsters – women with long swishy hair, who canter round the supermarkets and streets, eat grass-like substances and have a secret yearning for dodgy leather wear. Children, then as now, simply cannot distinguish between fact and fantasy. They read something in a story book, they see a film, and they are immediately drawn into the seductively dangerous worldview offered there.

The tragedy when I was growing up was that an innocent girl would read a pony book, find that the horse world was presented attractively, and the next thing you knew she was being sucked into

---

44. Though oddly, when I consulted a book called *The Five Stages of Becoming a Witch*, it didn't mention J K Rowling at all. It seemed to be mostly make-up hints, so who knows what danger lurks at your local Boots?

the whole full-blown gymkhana scene: hacking jackets, rosettes, the lot. Parents simply didn't know what their children were getting into. "I thought it was, well, harmless. You know, at least she's *reading* something, was my attitude. That can't be a bad thing, can it?" one woman said to me a few years back. "And then I started to suspect there was something funny going on. Eventually I found a pair of jodhpurs in her wardrobe and it finally hit home."

And now the whole horrible cycle is repeating itself. It was the same with little boys thinking they were steam engines or Batman. And they never grow out of it, you know. Most of us know adult males who still dress in fancy long cloaks and have a superhero complex.[45]

Biblical Sport of the Week: Bungee-jumping

This was boldly pioneered in the book of Acts by a young man called Eutychus. Back in those days they didn't bother with elastic, simply fell backwards out of windows during boring sermons. Don't try this one at home, kids!

---

45. In the church we call them "bishops".

"*Next time your mates get together, could you ask them to bring a duster?*"

Chapter 41
CRICKET 5 (FOOTBALL 40)

Martial Art of the Week

Tackling the School Reader

Both my sons wept tears of rage and frustration over their school reading books. The older found them inexpressibly boring and would only read them if allowed to sing them *fortissimo* in an operatic manner. The younger one struggled in silence, possibly because of a misunderstanding over what reading entailed. He'd got the idea from somewhere that you weren't allowed to look directly at the word on the page. Reading with him a few years ago went something like this:

> *Patient Parent* (oh, all right then, *Patient Father*): What does this word say?
> *Son* (glancing swiftly): Dog.
> *PF* (encouragingly): Nearly. Look at the word.
> *Son* (studying picture carefully): Cat?
> *PF:* No. Look at the word and spell it out.
> *Son* (staring up at ceiling): Do ants have more energy than us?
> *PF:* Spell it out! Come on, *look* at the word.
> *Son* (glancing at word for one nanosecond then out of window): Bear? Pig?

And so on.

A VIK endured many hours of this, until our son hit upon the strategy – when all else failed – of painstakingly decoding the symbols one at a time and seeing if, when strung together, they resembled anything he'd heard of. An incredibly long-winded procedure compared with lightning guesswork, and nothing like as interesting for him. But that's reading for you. Once you can read fluently you forget what the process of learning the skill is like – unless you go to theological college and are forced to learn New Testament Greek.

With hindsight I now realise that he is basically a right-brain-dominant person. This means he has all manner of strengths, but very few of them are rewarded and affirmed by the National Curriculum.[46] Reading, along with tying shoelaces, is a skill that the right-brained child acquires late.

Sport of the Week – Sea-fishing

The highlight of a week's holiday with another family in Mull a few summers back was a sea-fishing trip. This isn't a sport for cissies. I was a bit concerned about our younger son, who had been deeply upset a week earlier in the Natural History Museum to see that the butterflies had all been "crucified", as he put it. What on earth was he going to make of the barbarous cruelty of fishing? So many of God's little creatures hooked on vicious barbs, flapping helplessly, before being finally dispatched with an iron bar! How would I console him? What would he say?

What he in fact said was, "Oh, PLEASE, can *I* smack it over the head? Please? Please?" Ah, how they grow up and leave their mother's embrace, these sons. One week they are weeping over crucified butterflies, the next they are psychopathic spanner-wielding mackerel-murderers.

That night it was mackerel for tea. A VIK feels that he won't mind if he never has to gut another fish in his life. Oddly enough, the children didn't seem to have made the connection between the day's sport and supper, and one after another they cried, "But Mummy, you *know* I hate fish!"

---

46. Or indeed by me, if I'm honest, as I occasionally prize such things as tidiness over the joy of finding 4,000 A4 drawings of orc armies displayed on the sitting room floor.

Chapter 92
CRICKET 6

Feast of the Blessed Cessation of Football being the Sunday Next After Cup Final Day (or IKEA Saturday)

Extreme Parenting

Long Car Journeys

This is one of the things my sons hate above all else. But until a sound Evangelical version of astral projection has been invented, there are going to be long car journeys. They may be whiled away if you have enough forethought or imagination, however. Here are a couple of suggestions:

Caravan-spotting

Do the following names mean anything to you? Swift Challenger, Buccaneer Elan, Ace Rallyman, Elddis Cyclone? If so, I can confidently predict you've been stuck in holiday traffic with nothing better to do than read the names of caravans. I found myself wondering which deluded daydreamer thought up these names. They all seem to convey things like pride, speed, potency, sleekness, a rambunctious pioneer spirit – everything, in short, which a caravan is not. I suppose it's fairly obvious that calling your merchandise the Elddis "Laneclogger" or "Turbosnail" isn't going to work.

Sermon tapes

Perhaps you've never had to resort to this kind of thing in traffic jams, having had the foresight to bring lots of sermon tapes with you for those tedious contraflow systems. On a trip up to Mull once, we were lucky enough to have an excellent taped version of *The Hobbit* read by Martin Shaw. As time wore on we were increasingly impressed by his rendering of Gandalf. How deep and sonorous could he get? we wondered, until it finally dawned on us that the batteries were getting flat.

No, I'm sorry. I've tried, but I can't finish this section without posing the question, *What kind of person listens to sermon tapes on holiday?* When they could be reading caravan names? You will no doubt write and inform me. Good-hearted folk with a love for the Lord, or something. But here's another question, a nas-s-sty tricksy question, it is, precious (sorry, too much Tolkien): Do you sometimes want to take a holiday from being a good-hearted person with a love for the Lord? And if so, what is that feeling trying to tell you?

Interesting road signs

When you have reached the point where all the caravans you see are swaps, try looking at road signs instead. Here's one of my favourites:[47] "This sign is not yet in use." I think it has a mysterious Zen-like quality to it. This doesn't seem to apply to the electronic signs around Glasgow which were put to very good use as secular wayside pulpits. FASTEN YOUR SEATBELT. BE A COURTEOUS DRIVER. OBSERVE THE SPEED LIMIT. DON'T PICK YOUR NOSE. Well, this is better than the old faithful we get round our way: CONGESTION ON M6.

---

47. My all-time favourite has to be "For Sale: Farmer's Own Seed."

Chapter 93
CRICKET 7

Health Supplement of the Week

Chocolate

The health-giving properties of chocolate are well known, and those of us serious about our health are prepared to go on pilgrimage to Cadburyland, or, if we have time for a full-scale health retreat, we make our faithful way to Belgium. One year, concerned by our flagging energy levels, a VIK took a restorative trip to Bruges.

Bruges is a town for aimless wandering, par excellence. Before long we came to recognise the formative Bruges experience of arriving at the end of a street, looking blankly each way for clues, shrugging, then selecting a direction at random and heading off again for more happy wandering – only to re-emerge in front of a chocolate shop we had left only ten minutes earlier. Interestingly, it proves to be one of the few places to which girlie navigational skills are ideally suited. While a VIK was busy consulting maps and gauging the position of the sun, I was saying, "I'm *sure* I've seen those pistachio noisettes before..."

I'm pleased to be able to report that it *is* possible to have too many Belgian chocolates, but it takes a very dedicated type of person to reach this point. A person not unlike the present author, who, for the sake of research, is prepared to cram in those last three pralines, tamp them down, then lie queasily back with eyes closed until the saliva enzymes have done the job, moaning softly and thanking God that there are no children around to jump on her stomach without warning.

Sport of the Week

Slug-wrangling

This is a little-known sport, in the sense that I have just invented it. I can imagine nothing more loathsome. My hatred of slugs knows no bounds, and was not lessened by the sight of one very large black slug which was attempting to slither over the wire on the guinea pigs' hutch by weaving disgustingly in and out of the mesh in a mire of its own mucus. To what end, I could not begin to imagine. Let's not waste our time speculating about the mental processes of slugs. They don't have any. They are simply slime-covered alimentary canals. Neither was my loathing helped by the certain salad episode at a recent pub lunch, where a VIK spotted a grey slug – tiny, but perfectly formed – making its slow way across his plate.

When I aired this subject a couple of years ago in the *Church of England Newspaper*, I was inundated with helpful suggestions, most of which had to do with putting small amounts of beer around the garden in shallow containers.[48]

Well, we know now that it's coffee, not beer, that will see off slugs. This was the conclusion of research undertaken in the States a while back. So chuck your leftover coffee and grounds on your hostas. We can stop secretly using slug pellets when our greener friends and neighbours aren't looking. We need no longer be tempted to pour salt on slugs and watch them froth to death before our appalled, yet strangely fascinated gaze. Instead, according to the American researchers, coffee will merely cause them to "respond with uncoordinated writhing". Much more humane.

---

48. Well, it didn't take me long to see through that ruse. Pssht! (sound of can being opened) "Just putting some beer out for the slugs, darling. Tum-te-tum. Goodness! Seem to have rather a lot left over. Well, waste not, want not." You Evangelicals! Honestly.

"Drink drivers!"

Chapter 99
CRICKET 8

Extreme Academic Sport

Off-subject Erudition

This is an Oxbridge sport in origin, where it is still played enthusiastically, but nowadays you will find enthusiasts playing in most centres of learning. The important thing to remember is that manner is all. Content is important, of course. The more recondite your nugget of information, the better. It is the style of your delivery that will win you the greatest accolade this sport has to offer, namely, the snide hatred of your fellow players. Your style should be casual and off the cuff. Better not to play at all than to betray the fact that you've been mugging up. Essentially, you are seeking to let fall, in a totally natural manner, the fact that you are au fait with someone else's field of expertise.

Bonnie Prince Charlie

This is one of my little oases of knowledge in a desert of woeful historical ignorance. I was driven to a better grasp of Stuart history by the relentless questioning of my firstborn at bedtime when he was three and needed an urgent explanation of the Skye Boat Song. "But Mummy, who *was* the lad born to be king?" Either that, or he didn't want me to go back downstairs and abandon him to the snakes under the bed. How time marches on! I suppose before long it will be the naughty magazines under the bed that he's worried about. And time marches on in the life of maudlin Scottish ballads, too. "Carry the lad who's born to be king/Over the new toll bridge to Skye." The romance has gone out of it, really. These days his foes would not stand baffled on the shore for longer than it took them to have a whip-round for the toll fee.

Makes of caravan

See Chapter 42, above. This is a risky choice, though. It is all too easy for erudition to shade over into anorakism.

Quantum mechanics/string theories/uncertainty principle

These are all good ones to have in your armoury, especially if you are generally regarded by your scientific friends as a ditzy woman novelist / arts graduate airhead without two sensible thoughts to rub together.

Every so often I read science books of the "popularised" kind. The effect of the popularisation is that occasionally patches of coherence break through like sunshine from behind the cloud of impenetrable theory. The rest of the time, although I can understand (with the help of a good dictionary) almost all of the individual words, the sense still eludes me. The prose then operates, at its best, like rather beautiful symbolist poetry translated from another language – you are bombarded with brilliant flashes, glimpses of meaning; your soul quivers with some strange resonance and you wonder how much richer your life might have been if you'd bothered to listen in O-level physics.

Useful catchphrases for the academic bluffer:

- Why the false dichotomy?
- As opposed to what?
- I'm not *entirely* sure what you mean.[49]
- What was it Hegel said again? No, it's gone.[50]

---

49. To be said in a tone implying you can think of at least four possibilities, all of them fatuous.
50. It doesn't have to be Hegel, of course, any more than you need have any notion what he said. The idea is to create the impression you have momentarily forgotten what would normally be at your fingertips.

Chapter 95

CRICKET 9

in which falls Ashes Thursday

Extreme Everyday Sport

Dentistry

Those of us with a long memory snort at the idea that a trip to the dentist nowadays might count as an extreme sport. Hmmph! In *my* day they used to pin you down and gas you, and you'd come round with no teeth! Dentists have done a lot to improve their public image. Have you noticed how they say these days, "I'm just going to spray a bit of water in now"? Without adding, "Because that will stop your exposed nerve end smoking as I drill it with my high-powered drill."

My children have so far escaped the ordeal of fillings. My younger son is inclined to think that having silver bits in your teeth would be rather cool. "Does it hurt?" he asks me. How to answer! "Yes, it REALLY, REALLY hurts! So make sure you brush your teeth twice a day!" But then if he ever needs a filling, he'll be terrified. So I end up hedging my bets: "Well, sort of. Yes. A bit. Not really, though. But slightly, so brush your teeth! Although it's not that bad..."

Another parental challenge is the tricky business of controlling your offspring at the dentist. I learned the hard way that it's worth making two trips if I want to avoid having them crowd round the dentist, keeping up a running commentary while I'm having my teeth scaled. "Cool! Blood!" "That's not blood!" snaps the dentist, nettled. "It's just a bit of...staining." The real problem is your total inability to shout "Shut up the pair of you!" with someone's hand in your mouth. All I can do is shut my eyes and pretend I didn't hear them enquiring ghoulishly if he's going to drill my heart.

Perhaps the next stage will be to send them in separately and wait outside myself. That would put a stop to the James Bond dialogue when one of them is being tilted back in the chair. "Do you expect me to talk?" "No, Mr Bond. I expect you to DIE! Ma-ha-ha!" I could spend the time in the waiting room browsing through the copies of *National Geographic*, or, if I was feeling brave, the scary health magazines, whose sole purpose is to introduce you to a wide range of ailments you had no previous knowledge of, but are undoubtedly suffering from.

Domestic Sport of the Week

Defrosting the Freezer

Last week I defrosted the freezer, something I normally only do when I'm moving house. It wasn't entirely intentional, I admit. Someone had left a plastic spear propped against the plug and it had somehow switched the freezer off. This is a complete waste, I can tell you. I was planning to defrost the freezer one Sunday morning and miss church *as is the habit of some*. Still, at least I got to wash the kitchen floor painlessly. And I mopped the water up with towels waiting to be washed. Then all I had to do was wring the towels out, hang them on the radiators, *et voilà!* – freezer defrosted, floor washed and towels laundered – three domestic birds with one stone.

Chapter 46

CRICKET 10

Health and Diet

The Importance of Fruit and Veg

It is a truth universally acknowledged that in order for a foodstuff to do you good, it must taste foul. Indeed, foulness is directly proportional to the benefit derived. This is why we force our children to eat their greens. We'd known that for years, but it still came as a shock to read of an experiment done in Aylesbury Young Offenders' Institution. Violent offences fell by almost 40% among inmates who were given dietary supplements of vitamins, minerals and essential fatty acids.

Part of me felt like weeping when I read this. The idea that young people might be helped out of a cycle of crime and violence by something as simple as a balanced diet is a bit heart-breaking when you consider the wasted lives and millions of pounds poured into deterrents.

My practical response was to load my sons' plates with leafy green vegetables. It would save countless hours of court appearances, I reasoned. Five portions of fruit and veg a day, I told them firmly; and no, five petit pois doesn't really count, does it? The only good news here is that tomato ketchup apparently *does* count. Or it would be good news, if my children actually liked tomato ketchup. "I used to like it, Mum," my younger son once reminded me, "only you said it looked like a red slug and made me feel sick."

Well, I certainly don't remember saying *that*. Does that sound like the kind of thing I would say? The new word today, children, is "rhetorical". Can you say "rhetorical"? It means a question that

DOESN'T NEED AN ANSWER, and if it *gets* an answer, the person *giving* the answer gets no pocket money.

Extreme Relaxation

There are always going to be moments in our lives when we have overdosed on adrenalin and require some soothing and mindless activity, like watching paint dry. One of the things I like to do now and then is go to Coventry. I'm not trying to imply that this is in the same category as drying paint, of course. Stay with me and you will see where this is heading.

One of the things I like to do in Coventry is sit in Costas in Ottaker's bookshop with a nice cappuccino and observe the crowds passing in the square below. Last time I was there I noticed a kiosk which said, "Watch batteries changed here". How about that for a spectator sport? I mentioned this to a VIK and he immediately broke into John Motson mode: "He's got the back off now. The crowds are quiet. These Casios can be tricky. Oh, and he's done it! Now *that's* why he's the best battery changer in the country! Let's see it again on the replay!"

THE SEASON OF WIMBLEDON

(Colour: clergy, white; laity, purple and bottle green)

Chapter 47
TENNIS 1 (CRICKET 11)

A Theological Reflection on Tennis

How might our Sunday worship best reflect and celebrate the great truths embodied in tennis? When I cast my mind back to my own tennis-playing days at Aylesbury High School for Girls, the thing which stands out most is those heavy wooden racquets which required a press to stop the head warping. I imagine that if you showed a young person one of these they'd look at the screws and clamps and speculate that it was some kind of medieval torture instrument.

Compare these with the racquets of today. Now, I was never much good at tennis, my main talent being for hitting balls up onto the science block roof, but I reckon even I could manage to return a serve with a racquet head the size of a dustbin lid. These modern things cover about half the court, so as far as I can see, you just sort of hold it out any old how and the ball will ping off it.

Another thing that strikes me about modern tennis is the kind of noise emanating from the court during a match. The other day I could hear my sons giggling as they watched TV. I assumed it was the Simpsons, but it eventually dawned on me they'd got Wimbledon on. It was a match between two women, and it went like this:

Agh-Eeeeeee!

Oof!

Agh-Eeeeeee!

Oof!

until someone eventually won a point. In my day we didn't grunt. Nothing was uttered until a point was won – apart, perhaps, from my doubles partner calling me a moron, or the gym mistress saying, "If you do that once more, I'll knock *you* onto the science block roof!" And in my day the distinction between sports wear and clubbing gear had not yet broken down.

But how does this translate into worship? Wooden racquets and Aertex shirts with your name tape sewn on the left breast = robed choirs and organs. Graphite racquets and grunting as you serve = guitars and compulsory use of the word "awesome". My tennis experience is a *Book of Common Prayer* equivalent. It still retains a certain Middle England period charm, but by and large, times have moved on.

Extreme Anglicanism

Gardening

In most contexts gardening is classified as a leisure activity, rather than an extreme sport. Not so in Anglican circles, especially if you are a vicarage family who have a large garden, but neither the time nor the inclination to garden.

My predecessor was a keen gardener and parishioners occasionally like to mention this, not sharing my broad-minded view that convolvulus brings a welcome splash of white to the garden, and blackberries can always be used in crumbles and jam. These parishioners look out of the back window, sigh nostalgically, and say, "You should have seen it in x's day!" I think it is greatly to my credit that I bear x no ill will.

It is all very well to be a slob in your own garden, but the problem of convolvulus and brambles cannot easily be contained. It will spill over into other people's lives and gardens. They are a very good sermon illustration of sin, come to think of it. Perhaps of adultery in particular. I know perfectly well that our weeds are being heroically hacked back by our long-suffering neighbours. I am grateful to them, as I know that not all neighbours are as understanding. After all, people have been shot dead in recent years over hedge disputes.

*"If next door's Lily would do a bit more toiling I'd have
a chance to consider mine."*

Chapter 48
TENNIS 2 (CRICKET 12)

Extreme Anglicanism

How to Survive an Ordination Service

Part i) Ordinands

The first thing to remember is that most of your friends and family will fall about laughing when they first see you in a dog collar at the cathedral before the service. This hilarity doesn't express their deep-seated doubts about your suitability for the ordained ministry. It's just that until this point they hadn't really been able to visualise you as a vicar. It strikes them that you look as if you are auditioning for a remake of *The Thornbirds*. Don't worry. They'll get used to it. If, however, the bishop guffaws at the sight of you kneeling in front of him, you probably do need to worry. Alternatively, you could just guffaw back and say, "That's good coming from you, Pointy Hat!"

Part ii) Children

The average ordination service is at least one and a half hours long, so do make sure your children have something to occupy themselves with.[51] I set fairly arbitrary rules about what my sons are allowed to do to while away the time during church. Of course, in my day we used to sit motionless throughout 45-minute sermons, completely unentertained, apart from the occasional much-treasured

---

51. Firearms and incendiary devices are not recommended.

malapropism. I let them read or draw, but not play on their Gameboys. I'm not sure why I ban electronic games, really. The official reason is that they distract the people sitting nearby, but if the truth be told, so does drawing rude and amusing caricatures of the clergy, which is what my ten-year-old does. For example: a cartoon strip of a bishop who is bitten by a were-vicar, and at the next full moon his mitre turns evil and possesses him. When his secretary brings him a cup of coffee, the mitre devours her whole and burps the mug back out.

My older son just reads stoically until it's over. He joins in the hymns and the eucharistic prayer, though something tells me he hankers after more lively songs than cathedral worship typically offers. After a recent ordination, he was singing in the car on the way home, "I the Lord of sea and sky/This song's so old, I want to die/But the bishops think it's new/ What can we do?"

Personally, I'm a bit of a cathedral junkie. When the choir begin their motet, I lean back, close my eyes and draw in a deep and shuddering breath, like one who has just caught a whiff of the most ravishing aroma. Ah yes, these people are professionals. This is why we indulge them when, man and boy, they whip out their reading material as soon as the sermon begins. Well, that's why I'm prepared to indulge them. A VIK, being, one might say, a fellow pro, finds he is not as kindly disposed to them breaking out the thrillers and newspapers. I'm sure, as a matter of reciprocal professional courtesy, the choir would have no objection to the clergy reading (or getting out their iPAQs and playing a quick game of balloon-popping or patience) during those long tedious anthems.

THE SEASON OF MOUNTING DREAD

(Colour: black)

Once Wimbledon is over there is very little to disguise the fact that the awful Season of Football is bearing down on us again. Many Christians like to use this time as an opportunity to ponder the Four Last Things. Most of us, however, have no idea what these are, so we have to make do with a vague background dread.

When I was a girl this sense of approaching doom was quite vivid. Sometimes it latched onto such things as biology tests I hadn't revised for; at others it manifested itself in the conviction that a fox had got my pet rabbit. My default worry was that the Second Coming would happen before I was ready.

Every now and then it does us good to reflect that there are forces beyond our control. Football will come, whether we lead good lives or not. Fortunately, God is gracious and merciful whether we lead good lives or not, and we are encouraged to cast our cares on him.

Chapter 49

CRICKET 13 (FIFTH BEFORE FOOTBALL)

Sport of the Week

Map-reading for the Innumerate

I've decided that there should be special status given to the persecuted minority who are numerically challenged. We are discriminated against in almost every walk of life. Everywhere you go it's numbers, numbers, numbers. Take phones, for instance. I couldn't tell you off the top of my head what my parents' phone number is. I know it visually, but I have to be looking at the keypad. A VIK has hundreds of numbers committed to memory. I even know people who have learned their National Insurance number, for heaven's sake. And one of them *complained* to me that it wasn't a proper number, because it had *letters* in it.

The other place where injustice is deeply entrenched is in our road system. How am I supposed to remember road numbers, let alone junction numbers? Wouldn't it be easier if motorways were given proper names? The M1 could be, say, Dennis or Maureen. The M25 could be Steve or Karen. I don't know, what about Pinksniff Lilliballurum for the M6? At least that way I'd remember them. They'd take on personalities, acquire histories in my mind. And the travel news would be so much more interesting. "Traffic very slow anti-clockwise on Steve. Two-mile tailback southbound on Maureen at the junction with Arthur Blenkinsop."

Anti-sport

The Art of Idleness

Many people underestimate the quiet art of idleness. All these sporty types bustling around in Lycra tend to make us feel guilty and furtive about our idleness. The modern world is geared up to provide us with instant satisfaction. We demand it. In fact, we want it yesterday. Staring vacantly into space is a lost art. So is creative waiting.

We live in an age of labour-saving gadgets. We have this illusion that things can be done instantly. How often do we sit at our computers snarling, "Come on, come on!" as we wait some 40 seconds for it to do its thing? I try to remind myself of the time when I was writing an undergraduate thesis and had to send it to a typist, who sent back the typescript with two carbon copies. And I'm not even old![52] Or take the internet. People call it the World Wide Wait when it takes them ten minutes to access the information they're after. They must have forgotten about inter-library loans.

The saddest thing is what we do with all the time we save with our gadgets and high-tech equipment – we use it to squeeze in a bit more frenzied activity. I'm a great believer in slobbing about and doing nothing. If you want to give this a more positive gloss, you can talk about what God did on the seventh day. I think people are finding it increasingly hard to say to themselves, "That's it. I've done enough for one day."

---

52. Despite what my sons may think, I have no first-hand memories of World War I, the Irish potato famine or the Viking raids.

Chapter 50

CRICKET 14 (FOURTH BEFORE FOOTBALL)

Extreme Parenting

Summary Activities for Children

I had to hide *The Observer* from my sons one weekend last July. It had a big headline on the front cover which read, "£1,200 to keep your child happy this summer." I knew that as soon as they learned that this was the estimated cost of keeping a child occupied during the long holidays, they would demand that I hand over the money at once. After all, who better to decide what makes them happy than their good selves? No more salt dough and trudging round castles. Let's cut straight to Games Workshop for £1,200 worth of Warhammer.

This sum reflected the fact that in many cases parents are unable to take six weeks off work, and therefore need to make expensive childcare arrangements. That was what I was going to say if my children saw the article, before suggesting that they ought to pay *me* £1,200 for looking after them. Do I not make them nutritious meals, where a less devoted parent would send them out to forage for fizzy cola bottles on the floor round the Pick 'n' Mix counter?

A closer examination of the figures printed in *The Observer* revealed that the parents questioned were prepared to fork out another £100 on top of childcare "to keep their children amused every week". Come, come! There are many inexpensive ways of keeping children amused. Here's my favourite. Simply sit reading and eventually they will go away and find some way of amusing themselves. This is much better for the children. It teaches them to be creative. Boredom is the mother of invention. Having said that, my older son rather worryingly announced that he'd got a good look at *The Anarchist's Cookbook* in chemistry (these C of E schools, I don't know) and now knows how to make a hydrogen bomb. Plastic explosives, a couple of chunks of uranium, two pure hydrogen isotopes, a large metal tube to pack it in, fuse and detonator. "And that's it!" he said with an artless smile. "So simple – yet so effective."

Advanced Mothering Skills

Part i) Umpiring

One of the most tiresome aspects of motherhood is the endless umpiring it requires. I remember hearing once of a woman with four children. She simply designated a Victim of the Week who copped it for whatever misdemeanours occurred. Each child took a turn in strict rotation. In some ways this system is probably less arbitrary than the one I employ, which is to take no notice for as long as possible, then blame the older one. According to him. This is because I don't care what's going on, frankly. It is not a question of which brother is annoying which, so much as the fact that they are *both* annoying *me*.

Perhaps the way forward is to adopt the footballing model (or "mothballing", as my spellcheck urges. There could be something in this suggestion – simply put troublesome children into storage until they emerge as sensible well-adjusted adults). I think if I provided myself with a whistle and red and yellow cards, I'd soon crack the squabbling problem.

Part ii) Foresight and Vigilance

These skills are needed most urgently when children are small. You need to be able to scan a room and predict which apparently harmless object is most likely to inflict an unforeseen injury. It doesn't take mothers long to work out that where there is mud and water, there will be a small person tumbling in. When he was tiny, my younger son seemed to have the conviction that broken gutters are nature's way of providing you with an outdoor shower bath. So whenever I glimpsed water cascading from a rooftop some 50 yards away, I'd say, "No!" He would turn and look at me, his expression clearly saying, "Spooky! How could she possibly know I was going to stick my head under that?"

"Have you been storing explosives in the drainpipe again?"

Chapter 51

CRICKET 15 (THIRD BEFORE FOOTBALL)

Healthy Eating

This is something that every keen sportsperson takes seriously, whether they be armchair, cerebral or gruntingly corporeal in their approach to the great all-encompassing sport of Life. No exploration of this topic would be complete without a section on the Staff of Life itself: bread.

Bread

A while ago I spent a few days staying with old friends. They have a bread maker. Naturally, I know a lot of people who own one of these, but I had never lived in the same house as one before. It turned out that these machines make a wide range of alarming noises, the worst being the slow pulsing thud, possibly the kneading cycle, which sounded to me like a large animal – a bear maybe, or a moose – which has met with a ghastly accident and severed a limb. The poor creature is making its way with ghastly dragging thumps across the floor. As you lie there, you picture the smear of blood across the lino; you see it panting and twitching before summoning up the energy to heave itself one pace further. Or is that just me? Yes, it's probably just me. Normal people probably think, Oh, there goes the bread maker.

But the bread tasted good. I was already wondering whether the intolerable burden of having a wounded moose in your house would be outweighed by the smell of fresh bread each morning, when lo! I read the next weekend in my paper that those rascals at the supermarket are loading fat into our bread. "Three slices of bread have more fat than Mars bar," trumpeted *The Sunday Times*. The worst aspect is the fact that brown bread has far more added fat than white. We can't have impressionable children reading that. It would be like that awful day when my son saw an article stating that if you microwaved your broccoli it killed off all the nutrients. "So all these years I've been eating broccoli FOR NOTHING?!!"

It isn't just our bread that is being pumped full of fat, either. Cakes, biscuits, pizzas, cereals and meat dishes all have their fat content boosted, either to prolong their shelf life, or simply to bulk them up in much the same way as water injected into frozen foods. The fats involved aren't plain honest-to-goodness lard or butter, but scary mutant trans fats from Planet Cholesterol.

So here we raise a hoorah for home baking. Yes, a batch of homemade chocolate chip cookies has fat and sugar in – but it doesn't have anything like as much as shop-bought stuff and it tastes twice as nice.

Extreme Academic Sport

Plagiarism

When I was a student, back in the bad old days before the internet,[53] you couldn't just log onto an essay-writing service and buy 2,000 words on Keats for £50, like the youngsters can nowadays. This is scurrilous. It takes all the challenge out of plagiarism. In my era it was a tedious business of reading stuff up in books and journals, and selecting chunks to disguise in your own essay. The easiest it got was begging an essay from another student, but even then you had to copy it out laboriously in your own handwriting. No wonder standards are dropping. No wonder young people are all obese.

---

53. or the "interweb" as a crusty old friend of mine likes to call it. He also has a "personal wireless", so we can safely forget about him as a commentator on modern technology.

Chapter 52

CRICKET 16 (SECOND BEFORE FOOTBALL)

Extreme Beauty

Part i) Nailcraft

I find myself increasingly wondering what the correct Christian attitude ought to be on nail extensions. Up and down the country new Nail Bars are appearing on every street corner, taking up valuable sites which might be better given over to charity shops – unless of course, there is something wholesome and vital about nailcare which has hitherto passed me by. Gone are the days when all we asked of our fingernails was that they be capable of scraping labels off newly purchased glassware and squeezing blackheads. The era of grim functionality is past. We are now in the age of *nail art*.

As with any new development in contemporary society, the responsible Evangelical believer needs to ask what the Bible has to say on this subject. Well, as far as I can see, the only reference to nails is in Deuteronomy 21:12, and is part of the laws concerning the taking of a new bride from among defeated enemy captives. By all means, take her if she's beautiful and you fancy her, but make sure she shaves her head and pares her nails. Personally, I'm tempted to see that verse as culturally conditioned, but we all know about this kind of contextualising being the slippery slope to all kinds of licence.

Part ii) Walking in Silly Shoes

There was a time when I could party all night in three-inch stilettos. These days I can barely hobble 200 yards in my Cruella Deville shoes, as my sons call them, with their paltry one-inch kitten heels. I feel bitterly resentful about this, because my mum promised me while I was growing up under a strict regime of Clarks lace-ups, that I'd thank her when I was 40 and I still had nice feet. Even Clarks have proved unable to prevent KBT syndrome. That's a medical term, short for Knackered Big Toe. There is no connection between this condition and wearing silly shoes. It is hereditary. My father who passed it onto me has never worn stilettos in his life, being a Baptist.[54]

The one silver lining – apart from being able to demand taxi rides whenever I dress up – is that I *can* wear platforms, provided the heel isn't much higher than the sole. My mother never let me have platforms, so it was with immense satisfaction that I bought a pair in our local Shoepurmarket. The wounds never fade, do they?[55]

One of the things that help heal those emotional childhood scars is the support of good friends. One such friend, knowing about my poorly toe – sorry, *foot injury*, as we say at the dojo – bought me a pair of massage insoles. "Healthy & Beauty", the packaging proclaims, for "achy shoulder, constipation, achy waist". The insoles are made of clear plastic and have various little bumps which "can enhance the corresponding organs", for example, the "splenetic", the "secondary nasal cavity", "right windpipe" and the "pile". Just in case you're confused, the following clarification is offered: "There's different reflection vessels between humanbeen's organs and they also spread underneath the feet, which correspond to left or right organs."

---

54. I always think of killer heels as more of an Anglo-Catholic thing somehow, but that could be sheer prejudice.
55. There are women out there who never wear their hair in a fringe because they can remember their mum trimming it for them when they were nine, and ending up with a row of half-inch bristles, as Mum persisted in "just evening it up a bit".

CONCLUSION

The Big Wheel of the sporting year has made a full turn. We are back where we began, a year older, and possibly a little wiser, though equally possibly blundering about in pretty much the same way as we always have been. If we have learned something out there on the great Playing Field of Life, then our year has not been in vain. I, for example, have learned two things:

- always empty the vacuum cleaner *outside* after sucking up a plague of winged ants that have emerged through your sitting room floor
- the female praying mantis eats her mate while he is in the process of copulating with her

The challenge of learning new things is always *how to apply that knowledge.*

It would not be fitting to close this little volume without that most Anglican of things, a collect. So, for sportsmen and sportswomen of life everywhere, here is closing prayer:

> When the funny old game of two halves is over, grant us to
> know,
> that to be fair, we done good,
> we worked as a team,
> took the game to the opposition,
> and obviously,
> are literally over the moon.
> Because at the end of the day,
> credit where credit's due,
> it was all down to the Boss. Amen.

"Nope, I've checked, and there's absolutely no mention of a 'final whistle'."